'BETTER BEGGING THAN FIGHTING'

The Royalist Army in Exile in the War against Cromwell 1656-1660

John Barratt

'This is the Century of the Soldier', Falvio Testir, Poet, 1641

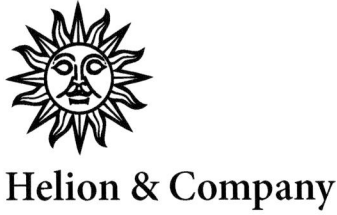

Helion & Company

Helion & Company Limited
26 Willow Road
Solihull
West Midlands
B91 1UE
England
Tel. 0121 705 3393
Fax 0121 711 4075
Email: info@helion.co.uk
Website: www.helion.co.uk
Twitter: @helionbooks
Visit our blog http://blog.helion.co.uk/

Published by Helion & Company 2016
Designed and typeset by Serena Jones
Cover designed by Paul Hewitt, Battlefield Design (www.battlefield-design.co.uk)
Printed by Hobbs The Printers Ltd, Totton, Hampshire

Text © John Barratt 2016
Images open source via author
Maps drawn by George Anderson © Helion & Company 2016

Cover: The soldiers of Ormonde's Irish regiment struggle off the battlefield. The five Royalist infantry regiments were to form up in three battalions. Two were either cut to pieces or forced to surrender. Only Ormonde's battalion, under the command of Lieutenant Colonel Grace, was able to retire from the fight in any form of order. Following the battle, the Royalist forces in Flanders were reduced to less than 1,000 men under arms. (Painting by Peter Dennis © Helion & Company Ltd 2016)

Every reasonable effort has been made to trace copyright holders and to obtain their permission for the use of copyright material. The author and publisher apologize for any errors or omissions in this work, and would be grateful if notified of any corrections that should be incorporated in future reprints or editions of this book.

ISBN 978-1-910777-72-5

British Library Cataloguing-in-Publication Data.
A catalogue record for this book is available from the British Library.

All rights reserved. No part of this publication may be reproduced, stored in a retrieval system, or transmitted, in any form, or by any means, electronic, mechanical, photocopying, recording or otherwise, without the express written consent of Helion & Company Limited.

For details of other military history titles published by Helion & Company Limited contact the above address, or visit our website: http://www.helion.co.uk.

We always welcome receiving book proposals from prospective authors.

Contents

Chronology		4
Introduction		5
1.	War with Spain	6
2.	The Armies	12
	The Army of Flanders • The French Army • The Cromwellian Forces	
3.	An Army in Exile	20
4.	Enter Cromwell	33
5.	Mardyke	50
6.	1658: The Campaign Begins	66
7.	The Battle of the Dunes	75
8.	The Fall of Dunkirk	101
9.	Aftermath	106
Colour Plate Commentaries		120
Bibliography		122
Index		124

Chronology

1635
May — Outbreak of Franco-Spanish War

1643
May 19 — French defeat Spanish Army of Flanders at Rocroi

1654
War between England and Spain

1655
April — Failure of Cromwell's 'Western Design'

1656
April — Treaty of Bruges between Charles II and Spain
October 8 — Stayner captures part of Spanish Plate Fleet off Cadiz

1657
March 23 — Treaty of Alliance between England and France
April 22 — Blake defeats Spanish Plate Fleet at Santa Cruz
May 1 — English expedition to Flanders musters at Blackheath
August — Capture of St Venant
October — Anglo-French capture of Mardyke

1658
March 28 — Anglo-French treaty renewed
May — Failure of Allied attack on Ostend
May 25 — Allies begin siege of Dunkirk
June 15 — Battle of the Dunes
June 25 — Surrender of Dunkirk
August 27 — Surrender of Gravelines
September 3 — Death of Cromwell

1659
March — Treaty of the Pyrenees ends war

1660
May — Restoration of Charles II

Introduction

The Flanders Campaign of 1657–59, which saw the army of Cromwell's Protectorate rather uneasily allied with Catholic France, at war with Catholic Spain, is one of the less well-known episodes of seventeenth century history. Still less remembered is the little Royalist army in exile, Irish, Scots and English, which had been raised to provide a core around which a new Royalist rising in mainland Britain could form, and to give the exiled Stuarts a little credibility as players in European politics.

The campaigns in Flanders and Northern France were frequently fiercely contested, climaxing in the Battle of the Dunes, when British troops fought on both opposing sides, and Cromwell's Redcoats gained a European reputation.

It was a victory which gave England a new foothold on the continent of Europe in the shape of the town of Dunkirk. One which within a few years the restored government of Charles II was eager to be rid of.

For King Charles II's men, said – not entirely fairly – to be 'better at begging than fighting', the Flanders campaigns were frequently times of hardship and privation. After the Restoration a few were incorporated in the new army of Charles II, but many, a political and religious embarrassment to the new regime, would end their days in the sands of North Africa, as part of the garrison of English Tangiers.

Thanks are due to the staffs of the Bodleian Library, Oxford, and the British Library for their help in researching this book. As ever all at Helion Publishing have been encouraging, imaginative and supportive in every step of the writing process.

John Barratt
Ludlow November 2015

1

War with Spain

There were a number of reasons for the outbreak of war between the English Commonwealth and Spain. Perhaps the most significant were economic; English merchants faced severe restrictions in trading with Spain's possessions in the New World, and indeed in Spain itself.

More important, though not openly voiced, were concerns which Cromwell and his Council had about the English Navy. It had until recently been fully occupied with operations against the Royalists, and the First Dutch War. But the conclusion of peace had left idle a large English fleet of 160 ships, which included among its commanders a number of political radicals, and an army of 12 horse regiments and 18 foot regiments. Keenly aware that they stood virtually alone in the face of a potentially hostile Europe, Cromwell's regime dared not take the risk of reducing its armed forces, but neither could they be maintained for long at their present strength. Quite apart from idleness encouraging political mischief, paying off a large number of ships and their crews would create more problems, as would disbanding many soldiers. War, preferably fought overseas, seemed an attractive alternative, and with luck might be self-financing. Employing the bulk of the navy, along with its more suspect commanders, away from home waters would also make any mutiny or insurrection less immediately threatening to the regime.

In 1654 England had two potential enemies, or alternatively allies, in the shape of France and Spain. Throughout the spring there was considerable uncertainty as to what course Cromwell would take. England might ally with Spain, already at war with France, nominally in support of the French Huguenots. She might side with France's Cardinal Mazarin against the longstanding Spanish foe or she might stay neutral. Both Spain and France, well aware of the financial problems of the English Protectorate, vied with each other in their offers of financial inducements. It seemed that the Lord Protector was awaiting the highest bid.

For Cromwell and the majority of the Council of State, war with Spain was the more attractive option. She was weaker than France, less likely, it seemed, to support the exiled Charles Stuart, and more Catholic. Ever since the days of the great Elizabeth, Spain had been regarded as England's 'natural enemy'. So war with Spain was easier to justify, and likely to be more popular with the nation as a whole. General John Fleetwood and his officers voiced the predominant viewpoint of the political and religious radicals, when they demanded 'What peace can we rejoice in, when the whoredom, murders and witchcraft of Jezebel are so many?'[1] If France agreed to expel the exiled Stuarts and offered toleration to the Huguenots, this, it was agreed, would overcome the main obstacles to an alliance.

The details of Cromwell's thinking are unclear, but he probably hoped to avoid full-scale war in Europe with Spain, and to confine action to the West Indies. He made two demands of Spanish Ambassador Carderas. These were that Spain should allow unhindered access to the English colonies in the New World, and that English merchants living in Spain should be afforded full religious toleration. The Spanish ambassador retorted angrily that that this would be asking his monarch 'to give up his two eyes', a response possibly founded on an over-estimation of Cromwell's desire for peace.[2]

Oliver Cromwell (1599–1658).

By July it was clear that Spain was unable to meet Cromwell's financial demands, still less to hand over the town of Dunkirk, which the English government required. War was now inevitable.

The English Council of State's hopes of cheap victories abroad led to the project known as the 'Western Design'. This was an ambitious scheme for a major amphibious operation in the Spanish Caribbean, involving a naval squadron and 3,600 regular troops from England supported by forces raised locally in the English colonies, notably in Barbados. It was intended to capture some or all of the key Spanish objectives of Santo Domingo, Puerto Rico, Havana, and Cartagena in the Isthmus of Panama. Equally attractive, given the Protectorate's parlous economic condition, was the hope that the expedition, through its conquests, would pay for itself.

With hindsight, considering the great distances and huge logistical problems involved, it is hard to see how Cromwell could have hoped for any major success. But there was a widespread tendency to belittle Spanish military ability. Former Dominican friar Thomas Gage, a principal proponent of the Western Design, assured the Council of State that 'the Spaniards cannot oppose much, being a lazy sinful people, feeding like beasts upon their lusts, and upon the fat of the land, and never trained up to war.' Even if this estimate was only intended to apply to the Spanish colonists, it left a great deal to be desired.[3]

News of the proposed Western Design led Spain to withdraw her ambassador from London, and to follow up with a declaration of war. This brought Cromwell's England and Cardinal Mazarin's government in France

---

1   Quoted in Austin Woolrych, *Britain in Revolution* (Oxford: Oxford University Press, 2002), p.505.
2   *Ibid*.
3   Quoted in N. A. M. Rodger, *The Command of the Ocean: A Naval History of Britain, 1649–1815* (London: Allen Lane, 2004), p.27.

'BETTER BEGGING THAN FIGHTING'

Robert Blake (1598–1657).

closer together in an alliance which at first was defensive only, though clearly more was to follow.

The war with Spain would bring none of the major battles at sea which had been a feature of the Dutch War. The greatest days of Spanish naval power were gone: knowing that they could not face the new English navy on the open seas, the Spaniards chose instead to mount privateering operations against English shipping, with Dunkirk a major base of their operations, and to place an embargo on English trade. In the meantime an English squadron under Robert Blake maintained a blockade of Cadiz.

Cromwell was pinning his greatest hopes on the Western Design. This ran into problems even before it set out, with bad relations between the naval commander, General at Sea William Penn, and his nominal superior, the land commander General Robert Venables; Venables was accompanied by his domineering wife, who frequently interfered in the conduct of operations.

The calibre of the troops was also mixed. Although most of the officers were capable enough, the ranks had been filled with undesirables of all kinds, with limited military capabilities. They were reinforced by 5,500 plunder-seeking colonists from the English possessions in the Caribbean, although the expedition was unpopular with the English merchants of Barbados, who saw it as interfering with their trade with the Spanish colonies. And, thanks to the incompetence of the committee in England with logistical responsibility, supplies and equipment were lacking.

In April 1655 the expedition at last arrived off the Spanish island of Hispaniola. The troops encountered considerable difficulties in making a landing on the rocky coastline, but on 14 April got ashore about 30 miles from the island's capital of Santo Domingo. The men were soon suffering severely from the effects of heat and thirst, having no water bottles and in any case with little fresh water available to fill them. Four days later, as they struggled through thick brush at the approaches to the town, the English troops were ambushed by a small force of 200 local *vaqueros* (cowboys). Panic ensued. Some of the officers fought and died bravely, and the 'sea regiment' formed from sailors of the fleet retained its formation, but the outcome was the total rout of the remainder of the English force.

Penn, whose ships had meanwhile been ineffectively bombarding Santo Domingo, re-embarked the surviving troops. The army officers were too disheartened to heed Penn's pleas for a renewed assault, and decided to try to salvage some credit by an attack on the island of Jamaica. The island, regarded as being of little strategic value, was only lightly garrisoned by the Spanish. On 11 May English soldiers went ashore, and six days later formal resistance was at an end although prolonged guerrilla resistance followed, with the English forces suffering heavily from disease and privation.

Penn and Venables, aware of the lack of hoped-for results from the Western Design, returned home with the fleet to face Cromwell. Both were committed to the Tower for a time, and Penn never re-employed. Jamaica would remain an English colony, used as a base for buccaneers and privateers operating against Spanish trade in the Caribbean, but the Western Design had proved to be a major disappointment for Cromwell's government.

It was clear that the war with Spain was going to be both tougher and less profitable than had been anticipated. For the moment emphasis shifted to the war at sea. A naval squadron of 'six nimble frigates' was stationed to blockade the Spanish coast and cut off the supplies of bullion from the New World on which the Spanish economy depended. In April 1656 a much larger squadron under Generals at Sea Robert Blake and Edward Montagu took up position to blockade Cadiz, but it was soon clear that the Spanish had no relish for a naval action. The English ambassador in Lisbon wrote home in frustration 'The Spaniard uses his buckler more than his sword. In the Dutch war we were sure of an enemy that would fight, besides good prizes to help pay charges, but the Spaniard will neither fight nor trade.'[4] In any case, the numerically respectable Spanish fleet was crippled through lack of naval stores.

However, by late summer financial desperation induced the Spaniards to take the risk of attempting to get that year's Plate Fleet through the English blockade. Blake may have withdrawn the bulk of his fleet to Lisbon in order to encourage the Spanish to take a risk. But off Cadiz he left a squadron of eight ships under Captain Richard Stayner to maintain the blockade, and on 8 September Stayner intercepted eight ships of the Plate Fleet attempting to slip into Cadiz unescorted. Six out of eight were captured or burnt, and Stayner took booty worth an estimated £200,000, although only about £45,000 of this found its way to the Protectorate's coffers.

It was, none the less, the first important English success of the war, and the English commanders learnt from a prisoner that the main Plate Fleet, with several million pounds worth of bullion on board, intended to make its way home in December via the Canary Islands. Cromwell rescinded orders that the bulk of the English fleet should return home for the winter. 'There can be nothing of more consequence than to intercept the Spanish fleet going to and coming from the West Indies, for which end our purpose is to keep a fleet in those seas, which may be able to fight with any fleet the Spaniards set forth, as the most effectual means to prosecute that war.'[5] Capturing the Plate Fleet would be a huge political boost for the Lord Protector: not only would its cargo pay off many of the Commonwealth's debts, but some of the international prestige lost as a result of the debacle of the Western Design would be recovered.

Cromwell, however, was never particularly knowledgeable about naval matters, and took an over-optimistic view of the profits which the war with Spain might still bring. He failed, for example, to understand that most of

---

4   Thomas Birch (ed.), John Thurloe, *A Collection of the State Papers of John Thurloe* (London: 1742), vol. v, pp.213–4. Hereafter *Thurloe State Papers*.
5   *Ibid.*, pp.563–4.

'BETTER BEGGING THAN FIGHTING'

The Battle of Santa Cruz. The defeat seriously damaged the Spanish war effort.

Spain's overseas trade was now carried in foreign-owned ships, so that, as Edward Montagu commented ruefully: 'we cannot hinder [it] unless we should fight with all the world.'[6]

Throughout the winter the now ailing Blake maintained the blockade of Cadiz. His main concern however was the Plate Fleet. Blake expected it to take refuge in the fine and strongly-defended harbour of Santa Cruz, in the Canary Islands. Here it could await intelligence of the situation off the Spanish coast, and hopefully the arrival of the fleet from Cadiz to escort the Plate Fleet and its cargo home.

In mid-April, after weeks of uncertainty, Blake learnt from an English privateer that the Plate Fleet was at anchor in the harbour of Santa Cruz. Knowing that the Spanish fleet in Cadiz was immobile through lack of naval stores, he decided to take the risk of immediate action, and leaving only two ships to watch Cadiz, headed for Santa Cruz with the rest of his squadron. He stormed into Santa Cruz harbour on 22 April, and in a furious contest sank 12 enemy ships and captured five, but failed to capture any significant amounts of treasure, which was safely ashore in the town.[7]

The victory boosted the prestige of Cromwell's navy throughout Europe, and, so long as a significant English squadron remained off Cadiz, the Spaniards dared not risk attempting to bring the marooned treasure home. As a result the Spanish war effort was crippled. A planned invasion of Portugal had to be called off, and Spanish forces elsewhere – including Flanders, most importantly for Cromwell – were weakened.

Blake died on 7 August 1656, as his flagship entered Plymouth Sound. His victory at Santa Cruz had given Cromwell momentary cause for optimism regarding a conflict which otherwise was not progressing as he had hoped. By the summer of 1657 it was clear that the Lord Protector's overall strategy had failed. Spanish privateers based in Flanders, especially at Dunkirk, were

---

6   Quoted in John Barratt, *Cromwell's Wars at Sea* (Barnsley: Pen & Sword Military, 2006), p.169.
7   *Ibid.*, pp.169–77.

doing serious damage to English trade. During the course of the war between 1,200–2,000 English merchant ships were taken by the Spanish, and mostly sold to the Dutch to replace the ships they had lost to English privateers in the earlier war. The bulk of Spanish trade was now carried in Dutch ships, which Cromwell dared not attack without provoking a new war with the Netherlands. It was time for a rethink.

2

The Armies

Both the French and Spanish Armies included large numbers of veteran soldiers. Both nations had been more or less continuously at war for decades, either in the ongoing Franco-Spanish War or the Thirty Years' War. The English troops who would take part in the campaign, whilst mainly newly-levied, were in most cases veterans of the civil wars in Britain. The small Royalist Army of Charles II was also composed of men with long experience of war, either with the armies of the Irish Confederacy, the troops which were raised in Scotland, or the English Royalist forces. Most of them had also then served with the French or Spanish Armies.

For a century Flanders had been something of a test bed for military techniques. Not only were tactics devised there, but it was also the place, later along with Germany, where soldiers learned their profession. By the middle of the seventeenth century the border areas of the Spanish Netherlands and its neighbours were studded with fortifications, ranging from the elaborate defences of key towns such as Dunkirk and Calais, through to hundreds of minor garrisons. With warfare often therefore being an affair predominantly of sieges, cavalry were at least in the Army of Flanders somewhat downgraded, although this would change when France rather than the Dutch provinces was the foe: 'we need more infantry if we invade the rebel provinces, and more cavalry if we campaign in France.'[1]

As it was, garrison duties tied up large numbers of troops of each of the combatants. On average around half of the Army of Flanders would be absorbed in garrisons. In 1639, for example, out of a total of 77,000 men, 33,399 would be manning 208 garrisons in the Spanish Netherlands. The large numbers of garrisons dictated much of the pattern of warfare in the region. As the Earl of Orrey famously commented in 1677: 'We make war more like foxes than lions, and you will have twenty sieges for one battle.'[2]

Most battles involved attempts to relieve a besieged garrison. This was the cause of the battle of Rocroi in 1643, when the French marched to raise the

---

1   Geoffrey Parker, *The Army of Flanders and the Spanish Road, 1567–1659; the logistics of Spanish victory and defeat in the Low Countries' Wars* (Cambridge: Cambridge University Press, 1972), p.87.
2   Roger Boyle, Lord Orrery, *Treatise of the Art of War* (1677), p.69.

siege, and a similar situation at Dunkirk would be the trigger for the Battle of the Dunes.

The Army of Flanders

At the end of the sixteenth century the Spanish army, and particularly the Army of Flanders, was still generally regarded as the predominant fighting force in Western Europe. Indeed it had demonstrated its ability through much of the known world, seeing action in the Low Countries, Italy, the Mediterranean, and the Americas. Defeat at Rocroi had badly shaken the Spanish reputation for invincibility, but the Army of Flanders remained an opponent to be treated with respect.

The Spanish Army was a multinational force, drawing its men not only from the wide range of Habsburg possessions in Europe – Spain, Portugal, Italy, the Low Countries and Germany – but also from a variety of other nationalities. At this time the Irish were the most significant of these.

It was felt that troops fought better when stationed away from their home territories. The Walloons for example, were generally viewed rather dismissively when serving in the Low Countries, but had a good reputation campaigning in Italy or Catalonia. The Germans were similarly viewed with caution by the Army of Flanders. However the 'native' Spanish troops were seen as the elite, reflected in their better pay and conditions.

Many recruits for the Army of Flanders, particularly those from Italy and Spain, had already received considerable training before they arrived. These elite troops were described as the 'sinews of the army'. Other troops, notably the Germans and Walloons, were normally raised by recruiting drives each spring, with a need to compensate for the high degree of wastage incurred on campaign, and through desertion and disease. The majority of the army's rank and file were men in their 20s.

By the 1650s, faced by war on several European fronts, Spain had serious problems raising sufficient men, and it was this shortage which made the Prince de Condé's Frondeurs and Charles II's Royalists a valuable addition to the Army of Flanders. Recruiters became less discriminating. In Germany Protestants as well as Catholics were now accepted, and much higher sums of money had to be paid to the collectors who recruited the men. The quality of recruits also declined. With compulsion increasingly used, magistrates took the opportunity to offload vagrants and criminals from their local communities. More use would also be made of men from the Walloon militias, who theoretically had only been intended for the defence of their home areas.

The Army of Flanders seldom had any problem in arming and equipping its men from the resources of the Low Countries and Germany. The tercio remained its basic administrative, though not necessarily tactical, unit. By the mid-seventeenth century the tercio was considerably smaller than had often been the case in earlier years, averaging around 1,500 men. A tercio was commanded by a *maestre de campo* and a sergeant major with a small staff. In theory a tercio had fifteen companies, though often fewer. Each had four officers and NCOs.

By the mid-seventeenth century, virtually all Western European armies had adopted, with slight variations, the tactical formations introduced by the Dutch and Germans. As in other armies at least two thirds of the troops in a company, sometimes more, were musketeers, and the remainder pikemen. Firing by file was generally used, though there is some evidence that as a legacy of the older tercio formation the Spanish may sometimes at least have formed ten ranks deep instead of the more usual six. By this time the lighter arquebus once favoured by the Spanish had been entirely replaced with matchlock and firelock muskets.

Until well into the seventeenth century the men of the Spanish Army had been noted for their flamboyant dress, but by the 1650s this had disappeared. The rank and file seem generally to have been issued each year with black felt hats, a coloured band identifying their unit, cassock and breeches, most often of brown cloth, two white linen shirts, a leather jacket, two pairs of stockings and a pair of shoes.

The war with France effectively closed the famous 'Spanish Road', the overland route along the western edge of France through territories generally favourable to the Habsburgs, by which troops from Spain and Italy had made their way to Flanders. This had been rather inadequately replaced by sea transport, using mainly neutral merchant ships, often Dutch. But even the largest of these could carry only a few hundred men. The entry of England into the war, with effective supremacy at sea, meant that it was now almost impossible to bring troops from Spain. Those already In Flanders were regarded as the backbone of the army, but there was an increasing shortage of infantry, with the result that the remnants of the Prince of Condé's Frondeur army and the Royalists of Charles II were a useful reinforcement. It also meant that the Spanish commanders had to make increasing use of the militia of the Spanish Netherlands, who on the whole were neither well-trained nor highly motivated.

Although the government at Madrid attempted close control of the administration in Flanders, the Captain General of the Spanish Netherlands and his largely military Council of War were in effective day to day command. The Captain General was normally appointed as much for his social status as for his military ability. In 1657 the Captain General was Don Juan of Austria, an illegitimate son of King Phillip III: Don Juan had commanded with some success in the suppression of the Catalan Revolt, and won some popularity from his pleasant personality, but would prove a somewhat lethargic and undistinguished general in Flanders.

Possibly more effective was his second in command, the Spanish general and political figure Luis Francisco de Benavides Carrillo de Toledo, Marquis of Caracena, Marquis of Fromista (Valencia, September 20, 1608–Madrid, January 6, 1668). He served as Governor of the Habsburg Netherlands between 1659 and 1664. Raised in a noble Spanish family, he made a career in the army during the many battles in Italy and Flanders between 1629 and 1659. He conquered the fortress of Casale Monferrato in 1652, and was Governor of Milan between 1648 and 1656. After the defeat of Don Juan of Austria in the Battle of the Dunes (1658), Caracena was appointed as his successor the next year. After the conclusion of the Treaty of the

Pyrenees, the Habsburg Netherlands had a period of peace. In 1664 Caracena returned to Spain, to assume command of the war against Portugal. He was unable to restore Spanish fortunes and was defeated in the Battle of Montes Claros, near Vila Viçosa in 1665. After the battle he was charged with treason and cowardice but defended himself by claiming that he was not to blame, and that the defeat was due to the poor state of the Spanish army. Afterwards, no longer employed, he died in 1668.

Charles II's Royalist Army in exile was partially reliant on the Spaniards for arms and equipment, as well as sustenance and medical care. The Royalists did purchase some munitions when funds were available, often provided by the Spanish; although at times they had a higher proportion of pikes, they were armed and equipped in the same way as other contemporary armies. Some attempt seems to have been made to provide individual regiments with distinctive uniforms: in 1658 the King's Regiment of Foot was issued with 'white' suits, probably undyed wool, but most of the army was probably dressed and equipped in the same style as the Spanish. Effective command rested with James, Duke of York, younger brother of Charles II. Aged 25, James had served with Turenne, and it was said of him that he 'ventures himself and chargeth gallantly where anything is to be done'. Later in life James was to prove a disaster in higher command, but in the fairly limited role he occupied in Flanders, bearing in mind that most of the details of his actions there are derived from his own account, James seems to have been competent enough.

Louis, Prince de Condé – one of the ablest generals of the era – was born in Paris, the son of Henri de Bourbon, Prince de Condé and Charlotte Marguerite de Montmorency. His father was a first cousin once removed of Henry IV, the King of France, and his mother was an heiress of one of France's leading ducal families. He was involved in many actions of the Thirty Years' War, taking part with distinction in the siege of Arras. He also won Richelieu's favour when he was present with the Cardinal during the plot of Cinq Mars, and afterwards fought in the Siege of Perpignan (1642).

His victory at Rocroi (19 May 1643) put an end to the supremacy of the Spanish army and inaugurated the long period of French military predominance. The Battle of Freiburg (August) was desperately contested, but in the end the French army won a great victory over the Bavarians and Imperialists, commanded by Franz, Baron von Mercy. As after Rocroi, numerous fortresses opened their gates to the duke.

The summer campaign of 1645 opened with the defeat of Turenne by Mercy at Mergentheim, but this was retrieved in the victory of Nördlingen, in which Mercy was killed, and Enghien himself received several serious wounds. The capture of Philippsburg was the most important of his other

Louis, Prince de Condé (1621–1686).

achievements during this campaign. In 1646 Enghien served under Gaston, Duke of Orléans in Flanders, and when, after the capture of Mardyck, Orléans returned to Paris, Enghien, left in command, captured Dunkirk (11 October).

His involvement in the rebellion of the Fronde eventually forced Condé and the remnants of his army to take service with Spain. But Condé's fully developed genius as a commander found little scope in the cumbrous and antiquated system of war practised by the Spanish.

The French Army

The French army went through considerable reforms following the end of the wars of religion of the late sixteenth century. The core of the army was formed around its standing infantry regiments, which were named after provinces of France. The first were 'Picardie', 'Champagne', and 'Navarre', with others progressively added.

The elite units of the army formed the *maison militaire* ('military household') of whom the best-known were the King's Musketeers (*mousquetaires du roi*), originally formed around existing units in 1622, and reformed as a regiment in January 1657. They were distinguished by their blue cassocks, edged with silver with a silver cross on the front. Other notables, including Cardinal Mazarin and leading nobles, also maintained distinctively uniformed guard units, though there was still no uniformity of dress in the French army as a whole. Grey coats or 'suits' were commonly worn by the foot. The French made much use of foreign recruits, notably Swiss and Irish. A saying was current that each foreign recruit was regarded as being worth three Frenchmen: one man for France, one less for the enemy and one Frenchman released for other work.

The normal tactical unit was the battalion, averaging 600–800 men, formed in ranks six deep, with the usual 1:2 pike:musket ratio. Depending on its strength, a regiment could form as many as two battalions or less than one. Battalions were organised into brigades, consisting of two to five battalions, formed in two lines.

Cavalry were similarly grouped into regiments, but fought in squadrons of 200. By the end of the Franco-Spanish War the French Army had 109 infantry regiments (including 30 Irish, Scots and Swiss) and 30 cavalry regiments.

France was fortunate in possessing two of the outstanding generals of the age. Unfortunately one of them, Condé, was fighting with the remains of his Frondeur army on the side of Spain. The other was Turenne. Sickly as a boy, from the age of 14 Turenne served with the Dutch in their long war with Spain, developing a particular interest in siege warfare. Returning to serve with the French, in 1634 Turenne took the fortress of La Motte, and was made a major general. He was a taciturn man, remaining calm in most situations. Austere in his own needs, he was noted for his care of his men.

Turenne was at war virtually continually from 1634 onwards, fighting first the Imperialists in the Thirty Years' War and then the rebellions of the Fronde. The year 1643 was one of notable French success. Condé defeated the Spanish at Rocroi, and Turenne captured Turin, and was made a Marshal of France. More recently he had campaigned, with mixed fortunes, against Condé and the Spanish on the northern frontiers of France, with neither side gaining the decisive upper hand.

The Cromwellian Forces

The English contingent in Flanders were all issued with the red coats by this time closely associated with the Commonwealth army. Rather surprisingly, they seem to have had a higher proportion of pikes than was usual. This may have been a temporary measure due to ill-founded concern about the effectiveness of Spanish horse. There is no suggestion in contemporary accounts that the English troops were lacking muskets once fighting began; it is probably safer to assume that by then they were armed in the customary 2:1 musket:pike ratio employed by the French and Spanish.[3]

Henri de La Tour d'Auvergne, Vicomte de Turenne (1611–1675).

Descriptions of the regiments being new-levied are somewhat misleading. They did include some drafts from existing units of the English establishment, and the majority of recruits would have served previously during the Civil Wars. Overall the English force was at least as experienced as the other armies taking part in the campaign.

The first general of the English forces in Flanders was Sir John Reynolds (1625–57). He joined the Parliamentarian army soon after the outbreak of the Civil War, and may have been commissioned as early as 1644; by 1645 he was a captain in Oliver Cromwell's cavalry regiment, and took an active and courageous part in the later campaigns. In the dispute between the army and Parliament in 1647–8, Reynolds was viewed as a radical, and briefly dismissed. Back on active service during the Second Civil War, Reynolds was promoted colonel and his regiment established as part of the army early in 1649, when it was earmarked for service in Ireland. It was involved in the Leveller unrest of the spring of 1649, but after the suppression of the Levellers it went to Ireland, where it arrived ahead of Cromwell's main expeditionary force and took part in the defeat of the Irish Confederates by the English under-General Michael Jones at Rathmines on 2 August.

During the Cromwellian reconquest and the mopping-up operations which followed (1649–52) Reynolds displayed an unusual flair for well-timed, well-executed field movements, and he was promoted commissary-general of horse in 1651. He was generously rewarded with confiscated Irish lands, and became a strong supporter of the Protectorate. In 1654–5 Reynolds seems to have feared that he might be chosen to command the

---

3   Parker, *The Army of Flanders and the Spanish Road*, p.94.

'BETTER BEGGING THAN FIGHTING'

Sir Thomas Morgan (1604–1679).

projected amphibious expedition to attack Spain in the West Indies, but the lot fell to the unfortunate Robert Venables instead. Reynolds sat as an Irish MP in the Protectorate parliaments of 1654–5 and 1656–7. He also helped to suppress a planned Royalist uprising in Shropshire, and was knighted by the Protector shortly after this, in 1655. He married Sarah, daughter of Sir Francis Russell, another Cambridgeshire landowner; her sister Elizabeth was married to Henry Cromwell. So he might seem to have become very much a member of the Protectoral inner circle. In 1657 a rather unenthusiastic Reynolds was chosen to command the English infantry regiments being sent to Flanders.

Major General Thomas Morgan, second in command of the English troops, was a Welsh professional soldier of great experience dating back to the campaigns of Sir Horace Vere in the Netherlands. By 1642 he was a captain in Dutch service, where he fought alongside George Monck and Charles Fairfax; in September he was back in England. Morgan was a captain of dragoons in Yorkshire under Lord Fairfax by March 1643, and after the defeat at Adwalton Moor in June, Morgan's troops held up the Royalist advance on Hull. After contributing to the Parliamentarian victory at Nantwich on 25 January 1644 Morgan was promoted major and was the chief engineer at the siege of Lathom House the following March. He was made a colonel in February 1645, and on 18 June 1645 – probably on Lord Fairfax's recommendation – he was appointed governor of Gloucester. In conjunction with John Birch, Morgan led the surprise capture of Hereford on 18 December. On 21 March 1646 he took part in the defeat of the last Royalist field army at Stow-on-the-Wold. For six years from mid-1651 Morgan was Monck's second in command in Scotland. He was appointed major general in February 1655, and with Monck played an active part in the Restoration of Charles II.

Undersized, pipe-smoking, and with a distinctive high-pitched voice, Morgan – though almost illiterate and signing his name with difficulty – was one of the most efficient officers thrown up by the Civil War. Although no innovator in methods of attack or strategic planning, he was a master of drills and siege warfare. Popular with his men, whose welfare was always his especial concern, he had an explosive temper and a susceptibility to flattery. At bottom a loyal and obedient professional soldier, he had no pronounced political or religious views, accepting changes of government with calm indifference.

Sir William Lockhart of Lee (1621?–1675) was the eldest son of Sir James Lockhart of Lee (1588/1599–1674) and his second wife, Martha Douglas of Mordington. Unhappy at school at Lanark, he played truant and at the age of thirteen ran away to Leith to sail to the Netherlands and enter the Dutch army. Having joined the French army, he caught the Queen Mother's eye and became captain of horse. When William Hamilton, earl of Lanark, raised a cavalry regiment for the Covenanters in April 1644, Lockhart returned to Scotland as lieutenant colonel. He served against Montrose and with Leslie in England until Charles I's surrender at Newark; in 1648 he fought in the army sent against England under Hamilton in support of the engagement with Charles I, and at the battle of Preston. His recall to service as general of horse on Charles II's arrival proved abortive, as Argyll sought to constrain him through a joint command with Baillie and Montgomery, and he refused to serve on those terms. When Charles invaded England, he offered his services as a volunteer; rejected, he indignantly declared that 'no king on earth should treat him in this manner'.

In 1652 Lockhart threw in his lot with Cromwell, and his rise owed most to his surprise second marriage to Cromwell's widowed niece Robina Sewster, on 2 July 1654. Following the Anglo-French treaty of October 1655 Cromwell sought alliance with France against Spain, and on 29 February 1656 Lockhart took command of the English force when Sir John Reynolds was drowned. A 'gallant and sober person', according to Evelyn, adventurous in youth, and a courageous officer, Lockhart was also a skilful diplomat and a capable governor, loyal beyond expectations of personal advancement in 1660.

Sir William Lockhart of Lee (1621–1675).

3

An Army in Exile

King Phillip IV of Spain (1605–1665). Often unduly influenced by favourites, Phillip's reign saw a gradual decline in Spanish power.

At the beginning of 1656 the English Royalist cause seemed desperate. With the failure of successive attempts to overthrow the Parliamentarian and Commonwealth regime in the British Isles, the exiled King Charles II and his dwindling band of loyalists eked out an increasingly poverty-stricken and hopeless existence on the Continent, knowing that only foreign support or some unexpected turn of events in England could restore their fortunes.

The outbreak of war between Spain and the English Commonwealth seemed to provide just such an opportunity. The Spanish government, involved in its war with France, saw in Charles II an opportunity to embarrass both of its opponents. The outcome, in April 1656, was the Treaty of Bruges between Charles and King Philip IV, by which the Royalists were promised financial assistance, and, at some propitious moment in the future, military aid in an invasion of England. As well as long-term political and religious concessions, Charles more immediately agreed to try to secure the removal of all English, Scottish and Irish troops currently fighting for France. Charles and his advisers saw in this an opportunity to form, in Spanish Flanders, a Royalist army in exile, which would not only give the Stuarts some much-needed military 'muscle' in Continental power-politics, but would also provide troops to support an uprising in the British Isles.

Apart from individual English Royalist volunteers and some Scots, the bulk of the troops currently serving with the French were Irish. Recruitment in Ireland, by both the French and the Spanish, had taken place for many years, but a major upsurge had occurred after the defeat of the Irish Confederates in 1652. Anxious to remove a potential source of disaffection, Cromwell agreed that the Irish Confederate commanders and their soldiers could take service with any foreign prince not hostile to the English Commonwealth.

AN ARMY IN EXILE

Edward Hyde (later Earl of Clarendon) claimed that upwards of 20,000 men took advantage of this offer, and although this was probably an exaggeration, enough experienced Irish soldiers took service in France to form eight regiments of foot, in addition to considerable numbers serving in Spain.[1]

The Royalists recognised that extricating the troops from France might be difficult. The Irish who had entered French service had done so on condition that they were bound to serve only 'until their sovereign the King of England should call them to his service.' Edward Hyde, the King's Secretary of State, warned James Butler, Earl of Ormonde – who was coordinating the extrication of the Irish troops – that:

> It cannot be doubted that France is most watchful about that nation, especially as the French know that the mere presence of the king of England in these parts is sufficient to deprive France of their service.' He feared that any premature move might result in the French 'not only … imprisoning all the officers of that nation, but … Violently destroying and imprisoning the men.[2]

Edward Hyde, later Earl of Clarendon (1609–1674).

King Charles' younger brother, James Duke of York, was serving with the French and had just accepted the position of Captain General with their forces in Italy. But he was now tasked with organising the departure of the Irish units to join the King in Flanders. In February 1656, following the arrival of Charles in Flanders, James related that:

> All the Irish colonels who had served in the French armies under Monsieur de Turenne and Monsieur de la Ferte, hearing of it, wrote to the duke of York to assure him that they were ready to perform, as good subjects and men of honour, whatever he should appoint them. He thanked them, and recommended them by no means to suffer their soldiers to pass into Flanders piecemeal or in small parties, although the Spaniards might invite them, on the occasion of the King's having retired into their country; and that they should keep their Regiments together, as much for the service of his Majesty when there should be need of them, as for their own advantage. Besides that their soldiers could not disperse themselves, so long as he was serving in France, without doing great prejudice to his private affairs, and that when it should be time to make use of their offers, he would advise them of it.[3]

---

1   See Pierre Goulier, 'Mercenaries Irelandais en Service de la France', in *Irish Sword*, 27 (1986–7) p.67.
2   W. D. Macray (ed.), *Calendar of the Clarendon State Papers preserved in the Bodleian Library*, vol. 3 (Oxford: Clarendon Press, 1887), item 483.
3   A. Lytton Sells (ed.), *Memoirs of James II* (London: Chatto & Windus, 1962), p.219.

'BETTER BEGGING THAN FIGHTING'

James Butler, 1st Marquis of Ormonde (1610–1688).

Ormonde instructed Lord Muskerry, in garrison with his own and the Duke of York's Regiments at Condé, that he should 'march with his regiment to such a place in Flanders as his next should make known to him, when he should receive half a month's pay for all the officers and soldiers he should bring along with him, and required him not to fail therein, as he should not be declared a traitor to his King and country, and abandoned as an unworthy person by all his old friends, who had formerly esteemed him to be a man of honour.'[4]

By August 1656, the Royalist plans were common knowledge; an agent of the Commonwealth reported to Cromwell's Secretary of State John Thurloe in London:

> Charles Stewart's emissaries are very busy in debauching all the Irish soldiers, and there is no doubt he will have them all, and that Sir, you may assure yourself, the army that Charles Stewart pretends to gather in Flanders will consist of such troops as I believe cannot be matched in all the world beside, and I am confident all Englishmen (that can but pretend to the lowest principles of common honesty) will abhor a conjunction with such a barbarous crew as they will be.[5]

Despite the fears of Cromwell's agents, the response of the Irish regiments to the Royalist cause was not entirely whole-hearted. On 19 August Ormonde told Hyde that he had gone to the town of Condé and passed on to Colonels Lord Muskerry and Sir James Darcy:

> To let them know that the King required them to come immediately with their regiments to his service, and that at present he desired them to guard the coast of Flanders against Cromwell. They have answered that they are ready to obey the King's orders, and serve whenever they may be required; but that, in order to quit the French service like men of honour, they must first obtain their passes, being bound not to leave without them … Which the Cardinal [Mazarin] had again lately promised them with means to go any place the King should appoint. No [considerations] can move them from this punctilio. They desire that the King's orders may be sent them for their coming away.[6]

Hyde was somewhat irritated. He had made preparations for the Irish troops to come to Bruges, where they would receive provisions and quarters, and 'does not understand why these gentlemen should ask for orders from the King, when they profess they cannot obey them till they receive their

---

4   Birch, *Thurloe State Papers*, vol. v, pp.319–20.
5   *Ibid.*, pp.386–9.
6   Macray, *Calendar of the Clarendon State Papers*, vol. 3, item 490.

passes, which it is certain the Cardinal will not give.'⁷

On 28 August Lord George Digby (the Earl of Bristol), who was tasked with liaising with the Spanish regarding the Irish troops, reported to Hyde that the Marquis de Caracena, Governor of the Spanish Netherlands, was willing to offer quarters and subsistence for the Irish around Arras, which they were to fortify, though there might be some delay in providing for them.⁸

As Hyde had expected, the French were reported to be 'much offended,' by these plans to draw off the Irish from their service, and on 11 September Mazarin told the Irish Bishop of Dromore that he doubted that King Charles, who had been well-treated by the French, would have any part in attempts to persuade the Irish to defect:

John Thurloe (1616–1668) became Cromwell's head of intelligence in 1653.

> But thank God, their solicitations are as yet fruitless, Colonel Muskerry and others having forwarded the letters which have been addressed them by the Marquis of Ormonde with new protestations of fidelity, and doubtless all of the same nation are animated with the same sentiments and his majesty the confidence he has in them by leaving them in the most advanced places. Colonels Dillon and Grace are no doubt satisfied with what has been done in regard to them, and the Bishop may assure all the rest that they will not be less considered. Will speedily send back his [Dillon's] Lieutenant Colonel to Monsieur Dillon [to give] all satisfaction for the regiment and officers; the King will take care that all the Irish in his service shall be well treated.⁹

Ormonde believed that Mazarin's letter was just an attempt to dissuade the Irish from leaving, and pointed out to the Irish colonels that the French had made an alliance with 'the murderers of their Prince [Charles I] and professed persecutors of Roman Catholics and destroyers [of Ireland]'.¹⁰

Mazarin now moderated his attitude. He gave Muskerry himself, though not his regiment, permission to join King Charles, and on 4 October the Bishop of Dromore reported to Hyde that 'the Cardinal told me on the 1st that he would give a pass to any Irishman who wished to serve his own King, but as yet they were only making recruits for the Spaniards, for whom Ormonde and the Chancellor were debauching them.'¹¹

Irish reaction was far from whole-hearted support for King Charles. Clarendon would claim that when permission to accompany their commander was denied, Muskerry's men, virtually in their entirety, slipped

---

7   *Ibid.*, item 492.
8   *Ibid.*, item 496.
9   *Ibid.*, item 516.
10 *Ibid.*, item 523.
11 *Ibid.*, item 551.

'BETTER BEGGING THAN FIGHTING'

George Digby, 2nd Earl of Bristol (1612–1677).

away in small parties to join him. But other sources indicate that a considerable number of his men remained in French service, and that the Royalist unit which eventually came under his command included a large number of new recruits from Munster. Several regiments which enjoyed 'very good conditions' in French service ignored the summons.[12]

The Duke of York was one of those who found himself with a dilemma:

> When it was known that the King of England was not only in Flanders, but that he had signed a treaty with Spain, all men believed that the Duke of York would also withdraw there. This Prince, who was used to speaking in confidence of his affairs with Monsieur de Turenne, was advised by him to write to the king his brother and offer to his consideration, that having served in France and received his education there, having moreover contracted friendship with the most considerable persons at the Court and in the Armies whose interest might one day be usefully employed for the advantage of his Majesty, he believed it would be in his interest to permit him to remain in France. Whereas by quitting it, he ran great hazard of losing both his friends and the interest he had there. He believed he could render no great service in Flanders where it was enough for the Spaniards that his Majesty and the Duke of Gloucester were there. Besides this, there had been no mention of him made in the Treaty [between Charles and Spain] and the Spaniards had not shown that they desired him to join them. If they should happen later to ask for this, his Majesty could secretly consent to his remaining in France, while appearing vexed with him for his apparent disobedience, which would satisfy the Spaniards, and this connivance would be known only to the person who should carry the proposition and bring back the consent … but the king, far from consenting to the Duke's request, immediately sent him an absolute order to come and join him in Flanders with all possible diligence. He at once obeyed, and the French Court consented.[13]

On the way, James had a close encounter with none other than Sir William Lockhart, the English Ambassador to France:

> On his arriving at the gates of Clermont, one of his servants whom he had sent before to hold the horses ready, came to tell him that Lockhart, Cromwell's ambassador, was there and was lodging at the Post House, which was the best in town; whereupon he gave this man orders to have his horses brought to the door of the Post House. The Prince on arriving had his coach stop, took out his boots, got on

---

12 Brendan Jennings (ed.), *Wild Geese in Spanish Flanders, 1582–1700* (Dublin: Stationery Office for the Irish Manuscripts Commission, 1992), item 2153.
13 Sells, *Memoirs of James II*, p.223.

horseback in the street and immediately continued on his way. There was equal surprise on both sides. Lockhart feared the consequences. He knew that the duke of York was as well-liked by the people as he was held in consideration by all persons of quality in the Kingdom, and that the English of Lockhart's party were equally hated by all men. These reflections alarmed him; he caused his horses to be saddled, assembled his men in the inn, and made them stand on guard with their swords and pistols. He himself stood at a window of the room which looked out on the gate above the street, having beside him the principal men of his retinue who like him were uncovered. This probable that he stood thus to avoid taking off his hat and not be blamed for remaining uncovered. His footmen stood in the Court at the bottom of the stairs. Now the coach having stopped directly at the gate facing the window, the Prince saw him, and before he could get on horseback, all the people having eagerly run up to see him, the least word from him would have made them fall on the ambassador. Lockhart was afraid but his fear lasted no long time and the Prince's departure reassured him.[14]

The Marquis of Caracena (1608–1668).

Despite continued reports that Charles could muster 5,000–6,000 men, in reality the Royalist army in Flanders seems never to have totalled much more than half that, and men came in slowly. On 4 October Ormonde wrote to Hyde, from Bruges, that 'the King now pays 400 men's support' and Hyde replied that he would rather they pawned their shirts to live, than be disbanded.[15]

On the same day, Digby wrote from Bossau to Ormonde that he had been driven almost crazy seeking quarters for the first Irish troops who had arrived at Bruges: 'the delay has been caused by the disorder of the Spaniards, through the loss of Aix la Chappelle, and by the advance of the French.' He hoped that the good quarters which had now been provided would make amends. Caracena had just told him that the Governor of St Omer had been told to give free passage to any who came with the King's pass.[16]

On 5 October Digby reported that quarters had been arranged at Bruges for 600 men, who would be transported by water. There was a scarcity of bread in the city. Don Juan had agreed that the King could try to borrow money for arms and ammunition in Antwerp.[17] By 15 October Digby was reporting on plans to raise a new regiment of horse and foot under the earl

---

14 *Ibid.*, pp.224–25.
15 Macray, *Calendar of the Clarendon State Papers*, vol. 3, item 549.
16 *Ibid.*, item 550.
17 *Ibid.*, item 552.

of Middleton for Spanish service, and Irish troops from Catalonia and Italy in French service should also be brought to Flanders.[18]

All the newcomers of course expected regular pay, and from the beginning this was a problem for the Royalists. On 24 October Hyde told Bristol that the King 'was out of the little money remaining for his bread', and had 600 Irish troops to supply. Although the quarters in Bruges were for the moment sufficient, within 20 days he expected that 'the body of men will be very considerable. Orders should be given to provide for a captain and other officers as soon as a company amounts to above forty men, and for a colonel and other officers as soon as a regiment amounts to above 300 or 400.' He believed that few regiments in the Spanish service were as strong as this.[19]

There were still some uncertainties regarding the attitude of the French. On 27 October King Charles wrote to Lord Inchiquin telling him to make what haste out of France he could. Muskerry had been to Mazarin and 'after much importunity' had been given permission himself to leave France, but not his regiment.[20] Three days later Lord Taaffe reported from Paris that Mazarin would not provide any of the Irish troops with winter quarters until he received 'a clear resolution about leaving' from the Irish colonels.[21] Eventually the French decided not to provide them, and the men of Muskerry's regiment took matters into their own hands:

> He no sooner gave notice to them whither they should come, but they so behaved themselves that by sixes and sevens his whole regiment, to the number being near 800, came to the place assigned them, and brought their arms with them; which the Spaniard was amazed at, and ever after very much valued him, and took as much care for the preservation of that regiment as of any that was in his service.[22]

The Royalists were continuing to encounter problems with their Spanish allies. By the end of October around 800 Irish troops had joined Charles: much fewer than he had hoped for. The Royalists placed the blame for this disappointing response on the Spaniards. The Duke of York claimed that the Marquis de Caracena had failed to fulfil promises of quarters and supplies, though Caracena himself had written that although he could give quarters to four regiments, as he had originally agreed with Digby,

> And his majesty might give command of them to whom he pleased … that they could not give winter quarters to any more new regiments at a time when they were obliged to cashier above forty of their old ones, and that whatever men should come over to the king, as well Muskerry's as others, must be aggregated to one of these four regiments, which were ground work enough for a body of four

---

18 *Ibid.*, item 573.
19 *Ibid.*, item 583.
20 *Ibid.*, item 586.
21 *Ibid.*, item 588.
22 W. D. Macray (ed.), Edward Hyde, Earl of Clarendon, *The History of the Rebellion and Civil Wars in England begun in the year 1641* (Oxford: Clarendon Press, 1884), vol. v, pp.70–74.

thousands of men, which was more than they could hope to see drawn together by his Majesty this winter.[23]

Though an ongoing shortage of troops during the 1640s and 50s made the Spanish value foreign contingents, they seem to have regarded the Royalist force with a distinct lack of enthusiasm. The Spanish government only agreed reluctantly to Charles' demand that his troops should swear allegiance to him and not to Spain, and they distrusted some of the recruits who came over. Another cause of friction was the 'poaching' of men for the new regiments from existing Irish units in Spanish service.

A particular cause of dispute was the regiment commanded by Colonel Richard Grace. Grace, who during the First Civil War had been a captain in Prince Rupert's Regiment of Horse, had then served in Ireland: where, according to the Parliamentarians, he was 'famous for his cruelties, and many bloody villainies'.[24] Grace had then raised a regiment of foot for Spanish service. But, according to the Duke of York:

Richard Grace (1612–1691). The only known portrait of Grace, from a newspaper of 1651.

> When his troops were disembarked to the number of twelve hundred, it was so [ill-used] that he lost the half of his men before he could arrive in Catalonia. He nevertheless served in the campaign with much valour, but having been placed in garrison in an important fortress on the frontier, on learning that the King his Master had retired into France and that the Duke of York was serving in the [French] armies, he resolved to quit Spain, where he had no reason to hope for better treatment than in the past, but he did not think that, they having broken their word with him, he was for that reason freed from the obligation of behaving towards them as a gallant man and as became a gentleman. He sent to propose to Monsieur d'Hocquincourt that he should receive his Regiment on the same footing as the other regiments of his nation that were serving in France, and on condition that he might afterwards serve his King wherever the King's affairs should require it. The offer was accepted, and he was earnestly desired at the same time to deliver up his castle. But he refused. He agreed only that the Marshal should send Cavalry on a certain day to a certain spot, to meet the Regiment. He then sent to the nearest Spanish garrison to give them notice that they should dispatch two hundred men to whom he would deliver up the castle when he marched out of it. But that they should have care not to send a greater number which might cause him to suspect treachery because then he would not deem it treachery to deliver the castle to the French when he should be obliged to do so

---

23 Macray, *Calendar of the Clarendon State Papers*, vol. 3, pp.311–12.
24 John Barratt, 'Adventures of Richard Grace', in *Military Illustrated*, 103, 2009, pp.27–31.

for his own security and his regiment's. The evacuation was completed in good faith. He marched out of one gate, while the two hundred Spaniards entered by another, and he found the French horse at the rendezvous which had been fixed.[25]

Unsurprisingly, the Spaniards were unenthusiastic about Grace's arrival in Flanders, and King Charles was forced on 1 November to send a conciliatory letter to Don Juan:

> [He] would not have ordered Colonel Grace to march hither with his regiment, had he known the Colonel was so much in the prejudice of his Highness; but believed it was wished that all the Irish, without exception, should withdraw from the service of France, and sent orders accordingly to Colonel Grace, with more than ordinary assurance of his devotion. He is far from excusing everything the Colonel has done, and will forbear to send orders to him in future, but desires Don Juan to consider what may be the consequences of excluding that person, when such pains are taken to induce the Irish to remain in the French service.[26]

Hyde was particularly annoyed by the Grace affair:

> After having maintained 800 men for one week, orders have only come for quartering 600, [Digby] must urge that the quarters be settled once for all, so that friends may be encouraged to resort thither as fast as possible, and then four such regiments will be seen in Flanders as have not been there these many years. Within these few days above forty, mostly officers and gentlemen, have come over from England. Will it be in anyone's power to bring over their men if such delays are interposed as those in Muskerry's case? But it is more wonderful that they should treat colonel Grace as they do, considering the value of the man and the number that are involved with him. The Spaniards must be told that those who formerly deserted their service did so in the belief that they should thereby better serve their king, And that they come back now because they clearly see that the contrary is the case. And if duly encouraged that nation [the Irish] will be entirely applied to the Spanish interest, whereas if upon this instance of Grace's there happen any obstruction, the Bishop of Dromore will have notable argument of new sermons for adhering to the French.[27]

Those troops who had arrived at Bruges were discontented, both with their quarters and with lack of pay. On November 6 Hyde told Digby that 'Sir Edward Walker [the King's Secretary at War] was sent to visit them, who found faults enough, which will be amended, and the King has appointed another muster on Saturday next, and will have some there to observe and remedy all disorders.'[28]

In an effort probably to hasten Spanish support, on 13th November Digby was told to tell Don Juan that Cromwell was becoming increasingly

---

25 Sells, *Memoirs of James II*, pp.219–22.
26 Macray, *Calendar of the Clarendon State Papers*, vol. 3, item 594.
27 *Ibid.*, item 595.
28 *Ibid.*, item 597.

unpopular in England, and that Charles intended to seize an English port before Christmas in support of a Royalist uprising. It was necessary to have 'forces prepared for any conjuncture, and therefore of forming the four proposed regiments of his subjects and assigning them quarters etc. The King desires to know what supplies of ammunition and arms etc. the Spaniards will furnish.'[29]

Two days later Bristol told Hyde that he had had 'a very gracious audience of Don Juan, who gave more positive assurances than ever that he will not be wanting to the occasions that may present themselves in England. Pressed home the business of the four regiments; the only difficulty will be about the numbers on which colonels and captains be allowed.'[30] Nevertheless problems remained. On 18 November Bristol told Hyde that he had spoken with Don Juan and convinced him 'of his error concerning Colonel Grace, which he would willingly repair now it is too late, the Bishop of Dromore having written to Lord Dillon that Grace's, the Duke of York's and Muskerry's regiments are shut up in Beauvais, whence it will be impossible for them to come in a body, but not by parcels, to which [Hyde] may encourage them, as also those of Bethune and La Bassee.'[31]

Sir Edward Walker (1611–1677).

Problems in finding quarters for the troops from France as they arrived in small groups, continued. The Spaniards would not grant the Royalists quarters for more than for four regiments, so the trickle of volunteers coming over from England would have to be absorbed by them. Bristol, tasked with this, admitted that the problem had 'almost made [him] wild' and although by 27 November he had procured quarters for another 1,000 men, he 'would rather have a month in prison than to have to procure the like again.'[32]

By December the new Royalist army was beginning to take shape. Caracena had quartered three of the regiments at Louvain, Leer and Damme, and 'the fourth at some little town in Hainault as near to the Scheldt as possible'.[33] The regiments were to be formed and ready to march within six days. As yet they had less than half their required numbers of captains, for places were to be kept for 'persons of merit not yet in view' who might come over from England. On 26 December Bristol reported that command of the Lord General's Regiment had been given to a veteran Royalist, Sir James

---

29 *Ibid.*, item 604.
30 *Ibid.*, item 607.
31 *Ibid.*, item 612.
32 *Ibid.*, item 625.
33 *Ibid.*, item 636.

'BETTER BEGGING THAN FIGHTING'

Henry, Duke of Gloucester (1640–1660). A convinced Protestant, who might, if he had lived, been an acceptable alternative to the Catholic James II.

Hamilton, while Lord Newburgh was to raise a reformado troop of 100 men as the nucleus of the proposed Scots Guards.[34]

The Royalists' activities were being closely observed by the agents of John Thurloe. On 9 January 1657 one of them reported that the Duke of York's Regiment was at Louvain, Lord Wilmot's at Leer, the Duke of Gloucester's at Middleburg, Ormonde's at Damme, three miles from Bruges. 'They are paid six stivers a day, with free lodging space.' On the whole, however the English agents were not impressed with the Royalist forces. 'The King of Scots is at a stand, for all he hath lifted a few men; he keeps them as yet together, they are about five hundred, of Irish the most of them are, some Scots, and some English. Who rely upon him, and cannot live otherwise.'[35] Another agent was equally disparaging: 'Take it upon my word, there is not in all 700, for they mutiny every day … their pay is so small, they cannot live upon it.'[36]

Nevertheless, as we have seen, by late 1656 Charles had begun forming his troops into regiments. The first to be raised seems to have been the King's Regiment of Foot, under the colonelcy of that vastly experienced Royalist veteran, Henry Wilmot, Earl of Rochester, with Sir William Throgmorton as lieutenant colonel. To anticipate, Wilmot died in February 1658, and command was then exercised by another experienced veteran of the First Civil War, Lieutenant Colonel Thomas Blague. The unit formed the nucleus of the King's Regiment of Guards, formed in about November 1657. Most of the officers and men were exiled English Royalists, in many cases former officers now serving in the ranks.

As the first raised and perhaps elite among the Royalist regiments, the King's foot might have been expected to have been the best equipped, so Charles' instructions for its organisation are interesting. Like the other regiments, it was to consist of 16 companies, the colonel's company having an establishment of 100 men, and the others rather weaker, with 60 each. It may be that this structure, rather than the usual 10, reflects a situation in which there were rather more officers available than rank and file. Eight companies were to be armed with pikes, and the remainder with pikes and muskets in equal proportions. By the spring of 1657, the regiment still reportedly numbered under 300 men.[37]

---

34 *Ibid.*, item 658.
35 Birch, *Thurloe State Papers*, vol. v, p.533.
36 *Ibid.*, p.521
37 *Mercurius Politicus*, no. 358, April 16–23 1657, p.1750.

Little information is available regarding colours and dress of the Royalist army. However in May 1658 the King's Regiment was to be issued with 300 suits of 'grey cloth'. This was probably in fact undyed wool, which may have been the cheapest and most readily available material. Similar clothing may well have been worn by the other Royalist units, particularly as the Army of Flanders still had no uniformity of dress. The Royalist soldiers, like the Spanish, probably tended to wear felt hats, white linen shirts and dark brown breeches and coats or cassocks.[38]

The Scottish contingent, mainly exiles from the 1648 and 1650–1 campaigns, with some later arrivals after Glencairn's Rising, formed a unit nominally under the command of Lieutenant-General Middleton, but because of his absence in Germany, where he was trying to raise troops, it was actually led by James Livingston, Lord Newburgh. Charles gave additional instructions for the organisation of the Irish troops who formed the bulk of his army:

> All our subjects of the Irish nation who are returned to the quarters near Courtrai, with resolution to serve us, be forthwith divided into three equal parts, to be distributed into regiments under the command of our most dear brothers, the Dukes of York and Gloucester, and our right and entirely beloved cousin the Marquis of Ormonde … in which division our intention is that such of them who served under our said brother, the Duke of York, and Colonel Muskerry, during the last campaign in France, should continue under his command, so they exceed not the third part of the whole number, and those that were of Colonel Grace's regiment serve now in that of the Marquis of Ormonde. It is our further pleasure that the men so divided be distributed by thirty in company to such captains as can appear they were actually in command at their departure out of France with regard to their seniority, which rule is likewise to be observed towards lieutenants and ensigns. And we will put such officers as cannot be present to be put in the head of companies, for want of full number of thirty men, to be provided for [as] half captains until their companies be completed. The like provision to be made proportionably for lieutenants and ensigns.[39]

Ormonde's Regiment, eventually 700 men, was the largest Irish unit. Command was actually exercised by its lieutenant colonel, Richard Grace. Less numerically strong, with perhaps 250 men, was the regiment formed by an amalgamation of the Duke of York and Muskerry's Regiments, and now commanded by Lieutenant Colonel Lord Muskerry. The third Irish regiment was that of the Duke of Gloucester, actually led by Lieutenant Colonel Lord Taaffe, about 400 strong, in the spring of 1657. A sixth regiment was formed when about 300 Irish troops who had been serving in the French garrison of St Ghislain near Brussels deserted to the Spanish side on the persuasions of the Earl of Bristol, and were formed into a unit firstly commanded by him and then by a Colonel Farrell. The Royalist army was completed by the Duke

---

38 See George Gush, *Renaissance Armies, 1480–1650* (Cambridge: Patrick Stephens, 1982, 2nd ed.), p.52.
39 H. M. C. Ormonde MS I., p.17.

of York's Lifeguard of Horse, 50 strong, mostly English Royalist gentry, and well-equipped by the Spanish. There were plans to form a regiment of horse under the command of Charles, Lord Gerard, but this was never completed.[40]

Though by the end of 1656 the Royalist troops had been placed in winter quarters and were being paid each Saturday, together with a loaf of bread for each man, problems continued. Charles was chronically short of funds, and discipline among the troops seems to have been appalling. The Scots incurred Spanish displeasure by sacking a church in Bruges and defacing an image. On 8 January one of Thurloe's agents reported:

> Those English that are among them follow their old wont of vapouring and carousing, bragging to be their own carvers of other mens' estates and fortunes, if ever they get but foot in England, at present there is a great feud betwixt them and the Irish, because they are the best treated here, as being likeliest to be most true to the Spaniard, and the most keen instrument against the Puritan Roundhead rebels.

While in April it was said 'of all the armies in Europe there is none wherein so much debauchery is to be seen as these few forces which the King hath gotten together, being so extraordinarily profane from the highest to the lowest.'[41]

On 5 May John Somers informed John Thurloe:

> The country is full of Charles Stuart's soldiers who are better versed in begging than fighting, being all ragged miserable creatures; within town they are the most importunate beggars and without, on the highway, sturdy. A month ago they mustered 4,000, the Duke of York's Regiment, near 800, and the Duke of Gloucester near 600, are quartered at Berges, near Dunkirk, Ormonde's Irish Regiment, 900 is at Carri, by Bruges; the English 500 under Lord Wilmot; at Sier between Brussels and Antwerp; the Scots 800, under Lord Newburgh at Bintzi, 10 miles above Brussels, Since winter, many of Lord Cranston's Scots have come from the Swedish army, one Captain Hamilton landed at Ostend with 64 officers. And a new army is to be raised under Lord Bristol, beginning with 300 ragged Irish, who came over from St Ghislain.[42]

---

40   C. H. Firth, 'Royalist and Cromwellian Armies in Flanders', in *Transactions of the Royal Historical Society*, vol. 16 (London: Cambridge University Press for the Royal Historical Society, 1902), p.713.
41   *Ibid.*
42   Birch, *Thurloe State Papers*, vol. v, p.493.

4

Enter Cromwell

By the spring of 1657, the Franco-Spanish war was heading towards an exhausted stalemate. France had been divided and distracted by the civil war of the Fronde, which continued until 1653 before the forces supporting Louis XIV finally gained the upper hand, and the Prince of Condé, with what remained of his Fronde army, joined the Spanish. Spain was in little better condition, with its own Fronde-style rebellion, and uprisings in Portugal and Catalonia, as well as the ongoing war with France in Italy and along the northern frontier.

Although during 1652 the Spanish were able to suppress the Catalan Revolt and push the French back across the Pyrenees, the Portuguese Revolt remained a serious and weakening distraction. In 1653, along the frontier between Spanish Flanders and Northern France, neither side was able to muster sufficient resources to take the field before July, and Spanish lethargy prevented Condé from bringing Turenne to what might have been a decisive battle near Péronne. The campaign of 1656 saw Turenne thwart the Spanish effort to take Arras.

The ongoing stalemate meant that English military assistance was increasingly important for France. For Cromwell too, intervention offered tempting prospects. The treaty of alliance signed in Paris on 23 March 1657 offered the possibility of removing the ongoing threat to the Commonwealth regime presented by the presence of Spanish and Royalist forces in Flanders, and also the prospect of regaining the English foothold on the European mainland lost with the fall of Calais a hundred years earlier. The treaty stipulated that the main objective of the Anglo-French army should be the capture of the ports of Dunkirk and Mardyke, which would then become English possessions. A force of 6,000 English troops would be sent to Northern France to serve as a separate body operating with the French, with half of their expenses paid by the English government, half by the French. With fears of desertion to the Royalists in mind, it was stipulated that none of the troops sent should be Irish or Scots.

King Charles was continuing to have problems with his own troops. On 9 March Hyde reported to Ormonde a quarrel between senior officers: 'As to the dispute between Sir E[dward] Walker and Colonel Grace about commissions, neither of them is capable of right reason.' Walker had always

'BETTER BEGGING THAN FIGHTING'

The Army of Flanders on campaign. The typical appearance of Spanish and Royalist troops during the Flanders campaigns.

had a reputation for pomposity and self-importance, and Grace was a strong-willed character.[1]

Efforts were still being made to equip the Royalist troops. On 10 March John Somer, one of Thurloe's agents, reported from Ghent: 'At Middleburg saw Colonel Hollis (who is commander of the English under Ormonde and Lord Wilmot) buying a thousand muskets and other arms. At Flushing there are many officers who have resigned service under the United Provinces in order to wait upon Charles Stuart, who however is so in want of money that he cannot pay his soldiers.'[2]

Hyde confirmed some of these problems in a letter of 16 March to Ormonde:

> Ormonde's Regiment, having received two months' pay, now complain more than ever on account of the deductions. Poor Tom Morley, who says that Ormonde appointed him to be paid as a lieutenant, which was promised by Colonel Grace, on Ormonde's direction, has now only been paid as a common soldier, which he takes very heavily … Untoward difference with the Governor of Daun (a person whom everyone magnifies for extraordinary civility) which Grace takes so ill that he will not go thither. The governor committed a captain of Ormonde's Regiment, upon failing in some application he made, he threatened to plunder the town, and the Major refused, upon the Governor's demand, to secure him. The King says that the Governor was to blame, in that he sent, not complaint, but an order to the Major.[3]

---

1   Macray, *Calendar of the Clarendon State Papers*, vol. 3, item 761.
2   Birch, *Thurloe State Papers*, vol. vi, p.238.
3   Macray, *Calendar of the Clarendon State Papers*, vol. 3, item 773.

There was a dispute with the Spanish commanders when the latter demanded that one of the Irish regiments be sent to assist in the siege of St Ghislain. According to the Earl of Bristol, Lord Taaffe sent only 100 men; 'the soldiers, however being wiser and dutifuller than their commander, the whole regiment is come hither, where Bristol has armed them, given them money, and well quartered them. The same has been done to the scotch troops. They are under De Marsin's command.'[4] For his part Don Juan complained about difficulties caused by Bristol!

On 24 March John Somer told Thurloe: 'The King's new levies are all disbanding for want of entertainment.' And at the end of the month he added that 'Charles Stuart's soldiers are disbanded, he has not many above 2,000 who are only paid two stives a day.'[5]

However in April Royalist morale was boosted when, as Somers admitted: 'Two [Royalist] regiments were at the siege of St Ghislain under the Earl of Bristol; the Earl mounted the works and called to the Irishmen in the town "What? Are you mad, to fight against your own King?" Whereupon they threw down their arms and the surrender followed.' About 500 Irish joined the Royalists.[6]

The Protectorate's English contingent to assist the French was organised during April. Of the total, 1,475 men were drafted from already existing regiments in England. The remainder were to be volunteers. But this did not mean that they were raw recruits. There was a large reservoir of experienced veterans of the civil wars available, and most of the men enlisted were from these. As the French army was strong in horse and weak in foot, most of the troops to be dispatched were infantry. They were uniformed in the standard red coats of the Commonwealth army: 'they had new red coats given them for the terrible name thereof.'[7] Unlike the usual English army establishment of two musketeers to one pikeman, the newly raised units were armed on a 1:1 ratio of musket and pike.

Command of the expeditionary force as 'captain-general and commander-in-chief' was given to General Sir John Reynolds, then commissary general of the army in Ireland. He had served with the horse throughout the Civil War, and was brother-in-law and trusted associate of Cromwell's son, Henry. At first he had only been offered the post of second in command, and had written on 14 April to Henry Cromwell, expressing reluctance to exchange his current position in Ireland:

> For the second command of 6000 foot on foreign service, which is the employment now to be conferred on me, but I have not accepted my commission and do hope it will not be proffered. I have offered to go with the title of Major-General of the said 6,000 under your Excellency or the lord Richard [Cromwell]. But I am not

---

4   *Ibid.*, item 783.
5   Birch, *Thurloe State Papers*, vol. vi, p.254.
6   Macray, *Calendar of the Clarendon State Papers*, vol. 3, item 790.
7   James Heath, *A Chronicle of the Late Intestine War in the Three Kingdoms* (London), p.720.

willing to serve under another nation and a foreigner, or at best a general but half an Englishman.[8]

Second in command was Major General Thomas Morgan, who had held the same rank in Monck's forces in Scotland. Morgan had served extensively in Europe and the Low Countries during the Thirty Years' War, and during the Civil War had commanded dragoons and the Parliamentarian garrison at Gloucester in the later stages of the war. Reynolds and Morgan were colonels of two of the regiments. The other four colonels were Alsop, Clark, Cochrane and Lillingston. Roger Alsop was the only one of the colonels already serving in the Army. He had been a captain in Thomas Pride's Regiment of Foot in 1647–8 and then Provost Marshal of the army. He had not enjoyed this post, and in September 1656 he had petitioned Cromwell:

> In 1650, during service in Scotland, you took me from my captain's place and made me Marshal General, though I earnestly desired to be excused, preferring actual service upon the enemy, but I took it in obedience to you, and you promised me a lieutenant-colonel's pay and preferment. Yet my pay has been less than a foot captain's, and my profits small. I have to keep horses, servants, etc, and have only the poorer sort of prisoners, who cannot pay for their quarters, nor pay fees, and I am £500 poorer than when I took the employment.[9]

Colonel Samuel Clark had served with the Dutch forces, along with his lieutenant colonel William Beadle. Sir Bryce Cochrane was a Scot who had fought against the English in 1650, but had previously assisted George Monck in the capture of Carrickfergus in 1648. Monck probably recommended Cochrane for his command in Flanders. Henry Lillingston is an obscure character who seems to have served with the Dutch after the Restoration, and may have done so earlier. Some of the regimental officers had served with Monck or in the other Parliamentarian forces, but others seem to have been newly commissioned.[10]

On 1 May the newly-raised troops mustered at Blackheath near Greenwich:

> This day here was a rendezvous of the new raised forces which are to go beyond sea, and (it is said) under the command of Sir John Reynolds. They were in all six regiments, stout men, and fit for action as was manifest at their appearance. Words of exhortation and encouragement were given them in a sermon by Mr Hugh Peters, exhorting them that when they come abroad they be sure to avoid the vices of other places, and to remember the virtuous and victorious military discipline of England, by which (through God's blessing) so many great actions have been performed at home. This wrought upon the hearts of the soldiers so, that they declared themselves with alacrity resolved to hold up the honour and

---

8   G. E. Aylmer, 'Sir John Reynolds (1625–1657)', in *Oxford Dictionary of National Biography* (Oxford: Oxford University Press, 2005).
9   M. A. E. Green (ed.), *Calendar of State Papers, Domestic; Commonwealth Series, 1656–7* (London: 1883), p.94. Hereafter *CSPD Commonwealth*.
10 Firth, 'Royalist and Cromwellian Armies in Flanders', pp.103–6.

renown of England abroad. Afterwards, five hundred being drawn out of each regiment, which made up the number of three thousand, there immediately began their march hence towards the seaside, being to embark at Dover, from thence to be transported to Calais. The other three thousand are disposed up and down in quarters, waiting further orders, which they expect some time next week, and then to follow their fellows.[11]

In another account:

The honourable Major General Kelsey and Captain Hatsel, being at Dover, by the direction of his highness and the Council, to take care of the embarking of the said forces, did on Friday and Saturday last week (having first given them a month's pay) put three thousand five hundred men of them on board; who at their embarking manifested a great alacrity and resolution, to stand for the honour of their nation in this undertaking. They were not long at sea before they landed at St John's Bay, which is about seven miles from Boulogne in France, where they were met by a person of honour appointed from the King of France to receive them; as also by the Governor of Boulogne with many of the French gentry, to entertain and welcome them in those parts. The said person of honour gave them (in his Majesty's name) very good assurance that whatever was agreed on should be faithfully performed, and nothing be wanting which might be for their encouragement.

Louis XIV (1638–1715).

The remainder of the 6,000 forces are expected by the French, and when they are arrived there is three months' pay to be advanced to them all. In the meantime, care is taken by that honourable person for the accommodation of them in their quarters in and about Boulogne.

Part of the forces which were behind, which were quartered in the road towards Dover, have received orders to march thither, where the like care will be taken for their immediate transportation.

Yesterday one thousand old soldiers were rendezvoused upon Blackheath, by Greenwich, very gallant men, who are advanced to complete the number.

The French expressed a great deal of joy and satisfaction upon the landing of the former, and they gave us a volley of great guns, for a farewell, at the return of our ships.[12]

Another account adds more details:

---

11 *Mercurius Politicus*, no. 360, April 30–May 7 1657, p.7760.
12 *Ibid.*, no. 361, May 7–14 1657, p.7796.

'BETTER BEGGING THAN FIGHTING'

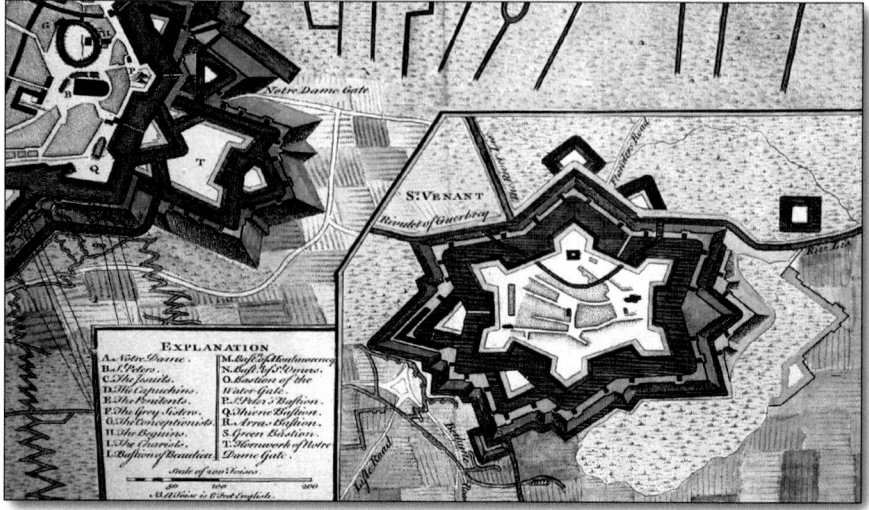

St Venant.

By some persons returned this day from Dover, we had an account of the embarking of the remainder of the new raised forces under the command of the right honourable Sir John Reynolds. Which was performed on Saturday last, and they safely landed near Boulogne, where the officers of the King and France lay ready to receive them, and disposed of them, in quarters among their fellows, in and about Boulogne, they making in all 6,000 men. The French declared much joy and satisfaction upon their landing, and it was expected that on Sunday night last the King and Queen of France, with a great train of nobility, would come down thither, in order to the viewing them on the morrow. Sir John Reynolds went from Dover, being shipped on Sunday in the evening, and Major General Morgan, a person of much honour and merit in military affairs, and in that respect fit to serve under so valiant and worthy a General, is within a day or two to follow him … so that we doubt not a good account will be given of this expedition, undertaken for the honour and service of this commonwealth in France.[13]

At first the English troops were on the whole well satisfied with their reception from their French allies. One officer wrote on 1 June from the English quarters at Rue, between Abbeville and Montreuil:

We are nobly treated, after the manner of this country, in all places, and hope the kindness will hold. We are quartered in their towns, and visited by their governors and magistrates. A gentleman comes each day to perform civility to our officers, in the name of the Cardinal. The king's own troop of gentlemen were divided by his appointment, and one half of them ordered to march before us. Wine and beer is plentifully given to our soldiers in each night's quarters. Our men, if sick or lame, are lodged in the houses of burgers; and indeed the French do give many demonstrations of really affecting our nation, and a union with it. We depend upon the lord for our success.[14]

---

13 *Ibid.*, no. 362, May 14–21 1657, p.7799.
14 *Ibid.*, no 363, May 21–28 1657, p.7809.

On 26 May, Captain Roger Whetstone of the English detachment wrote to General Monck:

'Our army consists of 6,000 foot, officers included, and hath been very civilly treated by order from the King and Cardinal. We have our ammunition bread with 5 sous a day per each soldier and are come thus far into the country being lodged in the strongest towns in France.' The 'boors', however, had taken to the woods killing and robbing all they encountered, and the English had lost three soldiers killed and several stripped and robbed by them. The soldiers were healthy, but 'water is so scarce here that we marched Saturday last above 10 miles without one drop. The Cardinal presents us with both wine and beer each town we come to.' Lockhart had assured the officers that they would be paid as agreed. 'We find a great want of cheese, which in hope will be supplied, brown bread and water being strange to our soldiers. The French treasurers niggle with us already stopping 2 sous for each pistol they pay us.'[15]

The agreed rates of pay for the English contingent were:

Commander in Chief	£30 a day
Physician	£6 13s.
Colonel	£12
Lieutenant Colonel	£6
Major	£5
Marshal	2 livres
Captain	5 livres
Lieutenant	2 livres 10 sous
Ensign	1 livre 5 sous
Farrier	16 sous
Sergeant	10 sous
Corporal	7 sous
Soldier	5 sous and ammunition bread[16]

Ambassador Lockhart, whilst praising the 'extraordinary kindness' with which the English troops had been received, suspected French underlying motives: 'something may lurk at the bottom of so much caress.'[17] The rank and file, whilst enjoying with relish the generous supplies of wine and beer they were supplied with, complained about the French brown munition bread they received, and with the lack of the cheese which normally formed a staple part of their rations.

The French were evidently anxious not to offend their allies. Lockhart informed Thurloe with satisfaction that:

---

15 C. H. Firth (ed.), *The Clarke papers. Selections from the papers of William Clarke, secretary to the Council of the Army, 1647–1649*, vol. II, p.84.
16 *Ibid.*, p.88
17 Birch, *Thurloe State Papers*, vol. vi, p.194.

I have settled the business of the march of your forces thus, they take place of all the regiments of the army save the two old regiments of guards; and care will be had that there shall be no occasion to dispute it with them, because their infantry will always march in two wings at least, and when the army is ranged in battle, the one will have the right wing, the other the left.[18]

Less well received was the scanty pay offered by the French to the English troops. They asked that the English government should provide them with threepence a day to bring them up to the usual English rate of pay. Even so, pay fell into arrears, and there would soon be desertions, in some cases to join Charles II's forces. The French also soon began to be critical, saying that the campaign had been delayed because of the late arrival of the English. Half of the pay was supposed to be provided by the French, though payments were spasmodic. Mazarin did provide 80 tents for officers, and two wagons for each regiment to carry baggage.[19]

About 11 June the English contingent joined the French army under Turenne at St Quentin, and on the 15th they were reviewed by Louis XIV and Cardinal Mazarin. Mazarin professed himself impressed: 'they are all well-made soldiers, and look as if they would do good service, and Turenne was equally pleased.'[20]

It was more than time to begin the summer campaign, and the French commanders decided to attack Montmedy in the Ardennes, with the aim of drawing the main Spanish field army away from Flanders. Part of the French army, under Marshal de la Ferté undertook the two month siege, covered by Turenne and the remainder of the troops; the English contingent formed part of the force under Turenne. He then swung suddenly westwards and after a 10 day siege took St Venant.

The English commanders, more accustomed to the recent warfare in the British Isles, where pitched battles had been more common, were surprised at the war of manoeuvre and siege carried on by the French and Spanish, and indeed their apparent deliberate avoidance of decisive battle. Reynolds wrote contemptuously to Thurloe: 'Fighting is not the fashion of the country.'[21] His disapproval increased when Don Juan and the Spanish forces moved as if to attempt to relieve St Venant, and took up position at Calonne on the River Lys, about a mile away from the besiegers. Reynolds asked Turenne for 2,000 horse, and said that with them and the 6,000 English foot he would fall on the Spanish camp, 'thinking that number of horse sufficient in that enclosed country, and relying on the bravery of the English foot, who had been accustomed to hedge to hedge fighting to supply their want of numbers.'[22] Turenne thought the plan too risky, and rejected it.

The English commander however, gained some satisfaction when 600 foot with great courage stormed the outworks of St Venant, and hastened the

---

18 *Ibid*., p.214
19 *Ibid*., pp.287, 290, 297; Firth, *The Clarke Papers*, vol. III, p.111.
20 *The Clarke Papers, op. cit.*
21 Birch, *Thurloe State Papers*, vol. vi, p.289.
22 *Ibid*.

surrender of the town. The Spanish had reacted by attacking Ardres, in the hope of diverting the allies from the siege of St Venant, so Turenne was able to march to the relief of Ardres. Reynolds told Thurloe 'I rejoice to tell your lordship that the taking of St Venant and the raising of the siege of Ardres, is wholly imputed to our English forces, of whom there is so high an esteem as is scarcely credible.'[23] Major General Morgan described the action:

> So that on the 26th following, Providence ordered me to march into the trenches with 600 men, and to carry on the point of the trench to the barricade which entered upon the point of the counterscarp. And having lodged 80 men to work into the ground there, we had a hot dispute with the enemy. The English courage, without the rest of the 600 men to see us engaged, moved them to leap out of the trenches to come up to us where we were upon plain ground, but our men shouting, firing, and crying "fall on" made me endeavour to get over the enemy's barricade and turnpike, which was soon broke open with the barrel of a musket, and so we entered within their counterscarp, and fell upon a half moon which was moated, and made the enemy quit it and enter the town, so that we wrought into a security, and our loss was 10 men killed, and not 20 wounded. Myself received a slight shot in the arm, which (blessed be God) since recovered with most of our wounded men. Marshal Turenne with most of the nobility in the army have had a high respect for us ever since. But indeed for the common and ordinary sort they are so blasphemous and vile both in words and actions, that it would make any that fear God unwilling to reside among them.[24]

The Duke of York had taken the field in command of the Royalist forces:

> Of 6,000 men in six regiments, viz. his own commanded by Colonel Muskerry, the Duke of Gloucester's by Lord Taafe, Marquis of Ormonde's, Earl of Bristol's, Lord Wilmot's and Lieutenant General Middleton under Lord Newburgh. The duke of York has a company of 50 horse raised by the Spaniard for his guard, in very good equipage, and they allow him 200 marks during the campaign for his table.[25]

According to James, when the French began the siege of Montmedy, on 22 June, the Spanish crossed the Sambre near Philippeville as if planning to relieve the siege, drawing Turenne to march to the support of the besiegers. But, James claimed, 'the real design was to beguile and deceive him' and fall on Calais in a surprise attack. A weak point in the defences had been identified, and the Spaniards had been considering an attempt for some time. 'They thought at last they would succeed and had taken measures so sound that it seemed the enterprise could not fail. It was conducted in such secrecy that the enemy had not the least suspicion of it.'[26]

---

23 *Ibid.*, p.299.
24 Sir Thomas Morgan, *The memoirs of Major-General Morgan. Containing a true and faithful relation of his progress in France and Flanders, with the six-thousand British forces, in the years 1657 and 1658* (Glasgow: R. Urie, 1752), pp.1–2.
25 Birch, *Thurloe State Papers*, vol. vi, p.304.
26 Sells, *Memoirs of James II*, p.228.

'BETTER BEGGING THAN FIGHTING'

Claude Lamont, 3rd Prince de Ligne (1618–1679).

But on 2 July when the Duke of York and his foot reached Arques near St Omer, planning to reach Calais that night, he received a message from Don Juan telling him that the enterprise had failed and he was to remain where he was. James explained:

The Prince de Ligne had been given command of an advance force sent ahead of the rest of Don Juan's force, and had marched from Gravelines as soon as it was night to execute the design at low tide by seizing that part of the town which was outside the walls and adjoining the quay, after which one could make oneself master of the town in twelve hours. But he arrived half an hour too late; the water was so high that it was impossible to pass through, and he was obliged to draw off having done nothing but give a sudden alarm to the town and show the governor where the weakest point was, which the governor then took pains to fortify and so deprive the Spaniards of any hope of being able to surprise the place.[27]

Some time passed in what James described as 'useless marches', before news arrived on 10 August of the fall of Montmedy to Turenne, who was now 'marching into Flanders to undertake some siege'. His objective proved to be St Venant, but by the time the Spanish reached Calonne on the River Lys, a league away, they decided that Turenne's position was too strong to attack. Instead they simply thought how they might cut off the enemy's provisions and prevent the passage of a convoy of four or five hundred wagons which they knew was to march next day from Bethune to the French army. It was judged fitting for this purpose to break camp and take up a position at Montbernanson by which place it was absolutely necessary they should pass. The country across which the army was to march being covered (with enclosures) and intersected with hedges and ditches, workmen were commanded to march at the head of each regiment with spades and axes to clear a way for them, so that the army could take up battle order in the plain which was only a cannon's shot from the enemy. The army was ready to break camp at dawn, and yet it only marched towards noon; the reason for this delay is all the more difficult to imagine because the success of the design depended on diligence. There was no neglect in warning Don Juan of this: the Duke of York advised him that the least delay would give the convoy an opportunity of entering the lines. But, despite everything that could be said, the army did not move until towards noon. The Prince de Ligne, General of the Cavalry, was at the head of the right wing, the Prince de Condé at the left, and the Duke of York, whom Don

---

27 *Ibid.*, pp.228–9.

Juan desired that day to perform the office of *maestre de campo general*, was at the head of the infantry. Don Juan and the Marquess of Caracena marched before with their three companies of Guards, until on arriving near the plain they wished to take their *siesta*, according to their custom.

The army could only move slowly in a country so enclosed. Nevertheless the Duke of York had but one enclosure to cross in order to arrive on the plain with the infantry, when he saw the enemy's convoy which, descending from Montbernanson, was marching with all diligence to reach the lines. The Duke, having passed the last hedge, put his infantry in order of battle; and seeing that the Prince de Ligne was also on the plain with four or five squadrons, he sent to warn him of the convoy's approach, and that he had only to go forward and capture it all, the enemy having but three squadrons as escort. The Prince replied that he could see the thing as well as the Duke could, that nothing was easier than to seize the convoy, but that he durst not attack it without orders from Don Juan or the Marquess de Caracena. The Duke then went himself to find the Prince de Ligne, and begged him not to lose so fair an opportunity by being too scrupulous. But the Prince replied that he knew not how far Spanish severity would go; that attacking without orders might cost him his head, especially if he did not succeed or if he should happen to receive the least reverse. The Duke replied that there was no ill success to be feared; that Monsieur de Turenne might indeed send out some cavalry, but that he would not venture to send his infantry out of the lines. He added that if the Spaniards should happen to trouble him about this action, he consented to take all the blame of it on himself, and that the Prince might justly excuse himself on the ground of having done it only in obedience to the Duke since the latter was that day acting as *maestre de campo general*. But all these reasons availed nothing with the Prince de Ligne. The opportunity was lost.

The convoy, which recognised the danger, redoubled its diligence; and when most of the wagons had entered within the lines, the three [Spanish] companies of Guards came to join the Prince de Ligne with orders to attack the convoy. He took with him only his own company of Guards. The Duke of York sent his. But the first four companies, which were led by the Count de Colmenar, Caracena's young and inexperienced nephew, marched forward so hastily and in such disorder that if the enemy's three squadrons had wished to dispute the ground, they would have beaten them. Berkeley, Captain of the Duke's Guards, seeing their bad manoeuvre, followed them in good order and was of great help to them, for the three French squadrons having been forced to hasten on, the Spaniards pursued them as imprudently as they had previously advanced against them, and engaged them pell mell even inside the lines, for the enemy had not had time to shut the barrier; but they came out more quickly than they had gone in, and fled without stopping until they had got behind Berkeley's company which had advanced to within musket shot of the lines. There they rallied, but became so prudent and phlegmatic that, without taking pride in keeping the post of honour which belonged to them, they left Berkeley the honour of forming the rearguard, and in this order they returned to join the army. This they found drawn up in order of battle on the plain, within a cannon shot of the enemy; where after remaining some time, it drew back a little to the rear and camped on Montbernanson. The enemy did not lose a single wagon of their convoy.[28]

Relations between the Spanish and Condé's troops in the army were strained at times, as James relates:

> The next day the Duke of York had a conversation on parole with the Marquis d'Humières and some other French officers who came out of their lines on purpose to find an opportunity of talking with the Duke. He had with him an officer named Tourville, who commanded one of the Prince de Condé's cavalry regiments. This officer was to have the guard with a Spanish regiment on the following day, at the foot of the heights that were within cannon shot of the French lines. He knew that the French would not fail to fire on them at daybreak; and so he asked someone of his acquaintance who were the Artillery officers in the French army. This man named them; whereupon Tourville asked him to present his compliments to one of them who was a personal friend, and to desire him to point his cannon at the Spaniards who were to be on his right and to be good enough to spare the left where he himself would be. The thing was carried out as requested. The Spaniards were regaled with quite peculiar distinction; they lost several men and horses before they were given orders to require, and not a single shot was fired on Tourville's squadron.[29]

With the failure to capture the convoy, and viewing the French lines as too strong to attack, the Spanish Council of War decided to besiege Ardres to draw off Turenne. After some delay, fearing an attack by Turenne, the Spanish army arrived before Ardres on 27 August, and despite that fact that the garrison was only 300 strong, spent a day and night constructing a circumvallation, which James regarded as 'very useless', complaining that an immediate assault would probably have easily taken the town. However the Spanish believed that St Venant would hold out for some time, and saw no need for great urgency. When a servant of the Duke of York's who had been with Caracena's trumpeter discussing some matters in the French camp reported that St Venant would fall imminently, the Spanish generals refused to believe him.

James now felt that he was getting the measure of the Spanish generals:

> This presumption and the negligence which had made them lose the opportunity of capturing the convoy that passed under their noses exceedingly surprised the Duke of York who was not yet accustomed to Spanish formalities. And this invites one to a digression which may come in here very appropriately, so as to cause less surprise at the faults they have been already seen committing and of those that will follow. Don Juan observed on Campaign the same forms of gravity and reserve as if he had been in Brussels. He was everywhere equally difficult of access. He and also the Marquess of Caracena, as has already been observed, were asleep very near the plain when the convoy was passing. Their servants who saw it coming down the hill,

---

28 *Ibid.*, pp.230–2.
29 *Ibid.*, pp.232–3.

as did the rest of the army, never durst awaken them to warn them of it. But what is still more surprising is that Don Juan and the Marquess, who both had much good sense and wit and bravery, could be attached to formalities. Which they well knew to be prejudicial to their master's service and their own reputation.

The Marquess was a very good officer, had served for a long time, had passed through all the degrees [of a commissioned officer] and owed his fortune to his merit; and had not Don Juan had, so to speak, the misfortune of being brought up as a Son of Spain [a son of the king] he was endued with qualifications which would have made him a great man. But their scrupulous formalities ruined everything. When the army was on the march, they never rode at the head of it, except when in the presence of the enemy. When half the troops were still out of camp, they would get on horseback and ride at the head of their three companies of Guards straight to the quarters which had been marked out for them, without troubling about the army, or taking pains to reconnoitre the situation of the ground or to know where the generals had their quarters. So in the case of an alarm or on the approach of the enemy, they knew nothing of the camp, nor where the main guard was, nor the advance guards. Don Juan was most often accustomed, on arriving at his quarters, to go to bed. He supped there and did not rise until the morning. When the army was not marching he seldom went out or got on horseback.[30]

However the news from St Venant, even if largely discounted, did spur the Spanish commanders into limited activity. They held a Council of War on 28 August, and from a nearby tower inspected the defences of Ardres through their perspective glasses. A fairly cursory examination decided them to make a limited assault on a half moon between two bastions, with the Duke of York's Royalist forces attacking the bastion on the right and Condé that on the left, exploding a mine to create a breach under cover of darkness.

The Duke of York and the Prince de Condé, not being satisfied with having seen the place from the top of the tower, went to reconnoitre it more closely. Don Juan and the Marquess did not go in person to reconnoitre where they were to attack, they only sent a Major de bataile to bring them an account of it, it not being the custom of Spanish generals to expose themselves on such occasions. All things being now ready, the army opened the attack as soon as it was night, on a signal from Don Juan's quarters. The besieged had no men to defend the approaches, and so the troops advanced to the edge of the ditch, where they secured a lodgement before attempting to attach the mine. For the Duke of York's attack his own regiment was employed. Lord Muskerry who commanded it had a captain and a few soldiers from other battalions to strengthen him. The Duke took care to send him fascines and everything that he needed, and then went to visit the operations with the Duke of Gloucester. He found that Muskerry had ordered everything as it should be, that he had almost finished his lodgement at the edge of the ditch, facing the point of the bastion, and that he had already lodged the body of the battalion in the ditch of the ravelin which covered the point of the bastion. The duke thought it was now time to attach the mine, but perceiving by

---

30   *Ibid.*, pp.234–5.

moonlight that there was water in the bottom of the ditch, he sent a sergeant to sound it, who reported that the water was not deep enough to prevent the passage of the miners. He sent them down into the ditch with a sergeant and a few soldiers to carry the planks by means of which they were to lodge themselves.

Day by now beginning to dawn, the Duke of York and the Duke of Gloucester withdrew and returned to their quarters. No details will be given of the other attacks; one may simply say that [if] they had had the same success and attached their mines, it was not doubted but that the place would surrender in less than twenty-four hours. Word was taken to Don Juan and the Marquess of Caracena, who were in their coach behind their attacking positions and out of cannon shot of the enemy, that the Prince de Condé and the Duke of York had been to view the operations of their own men. Don Juan replied: 'No hazen bien', which means 'They act not wisely'.[31]

Soon afterwards news arrived that Turenne had taken St Venant, and was now marching on Ardres. The council of war resolved to raise the siege:

The difficulty was to withdraw the troops from the attacking positions; there had been no time to make siege works and entrenchments, so they could only draw back in the open. The operation began by bringing back the miners, which was done in the duke's position by the care of Lord Muskerry. Before communicating to the officers who were with him any of the orders he has received, he sent word to the miners to return as best they could and that, to cover their retreat, he would have his men open heavy fire on the besieged. He caused his soldiers to believe he was withdrawing them because he had been warned that the place was countermined; and the miners, under cover of heavy fire from the musketry, reached the lodgement without mishap. He then told his men about the order he had received, and commanded them to retire, when he should give the word, with all possible diligence to a place he showed them, out of musket shot, where they were to rally. The Duke of York on his side ordered a lieutenant with thirty horsemen, to approach the place as near as possible without exposing himself until he saw the soldiers returning from the attacking position, and then to gallop among them in order to bring away any officers and men who might fall wounded. The Duke followed them to see his orders executed, and found that while his soldiers were drawing back from the attack, the lieutenant and his horsemen were stationed quietly behind a hedge within musket shot of the town. The duke galloped up to the lieutenant to repeat the order he had given. The other obeyed, and to make amends for his neglect rode to the edge of the ditch; and although the besieged opened heavy fire, no officers except Captain Knight and but a few soldiers were wounded, and none died, which was as fortunate as it was extraordinary. A few miners were lost from other attacks.[32]

The soldiers' problems were not over, however:

---

31 *Ibid.*, pp. 236–7.
32 *Ibid.*, pp.237–8.

After the troops had everywhere drawn back with very little loss, the baggage train was sent towards Gravelines, and the whole army followed. This march was extremely painful. On arriving at the edge of the lowlands, they were obliged to halt until the cannon and baggage were on the dyke or causeway which leads from Polincour to Gravelines and which the heavy rains had made almost impassable. The rain that continued without ceasing, the tempest, the darkness of the night, the road heavy with mud and the frequent halts they had to make, distressed the troops and threw them into so great a disorder that it was impossible for the officers to prevent their breaking ranks and seeking cover where they could. In the morning there were not ten men together in any one regiment.[33]

The fall of St Venant, despite the praise heaped on the English forces for their part in the operation, had done little to ease growing discontent amongst the English soldiers and their commanders. The French commented that although English behaviour towards the civilian population was better than that of their own men, they tended to be mutinous when their wants in pay and provisions were not met. During the siege of St Venant, Turenne had been forced to cut up his own silver plate and distribute the pieces by weight among the soldiers in place of coins.

The unaccustomed diet of brown bread made mainly of rye and bran, which was issued to the English soldiers, was alleged to have made them ill. Major General Morgan, never the most contented of soldiers, wrote to his old commander, George Monck, after the relief of Ardres: 'Since our coming into France we have had many hard marches, and being run in arrears of pay for six weeks together, our men being forced to subsist only with their ammunition bread, water, and fruit, it hath brought them into a great sickness and much discouraged them, insomuch that they make all the shifts they can to get into England, notwithstanding we take all the care possible.'[34] Some of the deserters joined Charles II's Royalist army, and were drafted into his regiment of foot.

Early in September, still pressing to be relived of the Flanders command, Sir John Reynolds told Henry Cromwell that he now had less than 4,000 effectives remaining from his original force of 6,000 men. 'Howsoever, if I must fight on until my dagger, which was a sword, become an oyster knife, I am content and submit.'[35]

Ambassador Lockhart had been complaining to Mazarin and Turenne since the campaign began regarding the strategy adopted. Early in the campaign he had objected to the French decision to lay siege to Cambrai, and, whilst acknowledging the care which the English troops were receiving from the French, pointed out that the treaty agreement under which the allies were to undertake operations against Mardyke and Dunkirk were not being kept. If this continued, it was possible that Cromwell would remove the English contingent elsewhere. He renewed his protests more forcibly during the siege of Malmedy. Lockhart pointed out 'the ill consequences

---

33   *Ibid.*, p.238.
34   Firth, *The Clarke Papers*, vol. III, p.385.
35   British Library, Lansdowne MS 823, f.104.

that were like to follow upon their delays [and] that the remissness of their procedure, in what concerned the keeping of their promises, did very much lose the affections of many persons of interest in England, who had hitherto always expressed great zeal for the alliance with France.'[36] Cromwell urged Lockhart to press English concerns vigorously, saying 'I desire you to take boldness and freedom to yourself in your dealing with the French on these accounts', and on 31 August told Lockhart to deliver Mazarin an ultimatum that unless there was an immediate advance against Dunkirk and Gravelines, the English contingent would be withdrawn:

> I am deeply sensible that the French are very much short with us in ingenuity and performance. And that which increaseth our sense of this, is the resolution we for our part had, rather to overdo than to be behindhand in anything of our treaty. To talk of giving us garrisons which are inland, as caution for future action, to talk of what will be done [in the] next campaign are but parcels of words for children. If they will give us garrisons, let them give us Calais, Dieppe and Boulogne; which I think they will do as soon as be honest to their words in giving us any one Spanish garrison upon the coast into our hands. I positively think, which I say to you, they are afraid we should have any footing on that side, though Spanish.
>
> I pray you tell the Cardinal from me, that I think, if France desires to maintain its ground, much more to get ground upon the Spaniard, the performance of his treaty with us will better do it than anything appears yet to me of any design he hath. Though we cannot so well pretend to soldiery as those that are with him, yet we think that, we being able by sea to strengthen and secure his siege, and to reinforce it as we please by sea, the best time to besiege that place will be now, and the enemy being in a capacity to do nothing to relieve it. Especially if we consider that the French horse will be able so to ruin Flanders as that no succour can be brought to relieve the place; and that the French army and our own will have constant relief, as far as England and France can give it, without any matter of impediment, especially considering the Dutch are now engaged to the southward as much as they can.
>
> I desire you to let him know, that Englishmen have had so good experience of winter conditions, they are confident, that if the Spaniard shall keep the field, as he cannot impede this work, so neither will he be able to attack anything towards France with a possibility of retreat. And what do all delays signify, but the giving the Spaniard opportunity the more to reinforce himself another summer to serve the French, without any colour of a reciprocal, or any advantage to ourselves.
>
> And therefore, if this will not be listened unto, I desire that things may be considered of to give us satisfaction for the great expense we have been at with our naval forces and otherwise, which out of an honourable and honest aim on our part hath been done, that we might answer our engagements. And that consideration may be had how our men may be put in a posture to be returned to us, whom we hope we shall employ to a better purpose than to have them continue where they are.[37]

---

36   Birch, *Thurloe State Papers*, vol. vi, p.504.
37   *Ibid*., pp.522, 824; Firth, *The Clarke Papers*, vol. III, p.119.

Lockhart delivered at least the gist of Cromwell's ultimatum to Mazarin, but Turenne, in what may always have been his intention, following the relief of Ardres moved on towards the coast; his plan being to begin operations against the ports, and if possible draw the Spaniards into battle. On 13 September Reynolds informed Cromwell of the move, and asked Admiral Montagu, commanding the English squadron in the Downs, to blockade Mardyke and Dunkirk. The English government were asked to dispatch siege and mortar pieces, and biscuit and hay as emergency supplies for men and horses in case the lines of communication with France were blocked. Reynolds also requested 3,000 reinforcements for his dwindling army.

Taslon, the *intendent* of the French army, came over to London to discuss with Cromwell and the French ambassador, Bordeaux, plans for future operations. Turenne said that it was too late in the campaigning season to do more than besiege Mardyke. Cromwell was most unhappy with this suggestion, and vented his spleen on Bordeaux in a stormy interview. Too much time had been wasted earlier in the year. Mardyke would require considerable expenditure in men and materials to be maintained on its own as a garrison. Bordeaux, for his part, defended the French decision at the start of the campaign to besiege Montmedy which had been intended, he claimed, to draw the Spanish Army of Flanders away from the coast. The capture of St Venant had secured the crossing of the River Lys, and enabled the French to take Burbourg, opening the way for a move against Dunkirk and Gravelines. But both were too strong to be attacked as long as the Spanish field army lay behind the Bergues–Dunkirk canal. The first step, Turenne felt, should be to take Mardyke, whose possession was necessary before the siege of Dunkirk could begin. Cromwell remained unsatisfied, but agreed to send 2,000 reinforcements to the English army. At the same time, a squadron of 25 ships would join an attack on Mardyke.

5

Mardyke

The Spanish army had been quartered at Drinkham and in the surrounding villages, recovering from their march from Ardres. After some marching and countermarching over the following few days, they took up position to hold the line of the River Colme, but on 17 September, learning that Turenne had crossed the river at Linck, the Spanish pulled back. The native Spanish regiments, with some cavalry, were sent to strengthen the garrison of Gravelines. Three Italian regiments under Don Tito del Prato were sent to defend the fort at Mardyke, and the remainder of the army was positioned behind the Bergue–Dunkirk Canal. The forces under the Prince of Condé were at Bergue, Don Juan at Dunkirk and the Duke of York at Odekerke, and the guns placed in already prepared batteries.

Mardyke was important as the site of one of the best harbours along that part of the coast. The defences of what was only a small village consisted of a stone fort with earthen outworks, and a wooden fort built on piles near the shoreline. Turenne appeared before Mardyke on 29 September and opened his siegeworks, blocking the route between Mardyke and Dunkirk, and began his bombardment. When the siege began:

> The Duke of York, who was intending to observe the enemy when they arrived before Mardyke, took with him the Horse Guards who were outside the gates of Dunkirk and advancing to within cannon shot [of Mardyke], he left the Guards behind to secure his retreat in case he should be pursued. He then, with fifteen officers and other men well mounted, rode up so near the French army, that some officers of the Regiment of Picardy, which was on the march, advanced some way and fired on him with the carbines they were carrying when on horseback. When they reached the quarter which had been assigned them and the soldiers began to build their huts, these officers and several from other regiments rode out again to drive back the Duke. But some of them who came nearer this Prince recognized a big greyhound they had seen with him in France and asked if the Duke of York was there. When they were told that he was, they cries out 'Sur parole', desiring to speak with him. He then stopped, and found among them several persons of the first quality who were all of old acquaintance. They alighted from their horses; the Prince did the same; and they conversed together for nearly an hour until Monsieur de Turenne ordered them to come back. There were quite two or

three hundred officers; the Marquis d'Humières, the Comte de Guiche, Castelnau, indeed most of the persons of quality and notable officers in the French army. The Duke of York had no more than twenty persons with him. Among whom was a Spanish officer of horse who, seeing him turn back when he heard himself named, was surprised, and asked him what he intended to do. The Duke ordered him to remain beside him, and said that no one had anything to fear.

This episode is related particularly that it may be observed what civility is used in that country even between enemies or persons of opposed parties, and that the Duke, although in the service of Spain, had no fewer friends in the French army. Some English who were present at this conversation wished to follow the same example, and they fared ill for it as will be seen hereafter. The Duke does not positively know whether the Spaniards took umbrage at these courtesies, but at the end of the campaign Monsieur de Marsin advised him, personally, to abstain from them henceforth. He told him that the Spanish character is suspicious and circumspect; and that, although they gave no sign of it, they might not be at all satisfied. The Duke replied that if his behaviour aroused their disquiet, they were very much in the wrong; that they had been unable to observe in his conduct throughout the campaign anything but great fidelity and application in their service; that he would always continue in the same way, and that in the event of a fight he would attack anyone of his acquaintance in the same way as even the most zealous Spaniard might do. But, he added, as for conversing when opportunity offered with persons who had served so long with him, he thought he could give himself this satisfaction without being of prejudice to the Spaniards; and that, to show them that he had no other intention than of following the customs of ordinary civility, he had not suffered any of the Prince of Conde's officers to be with him on such occasions, because he did not think it reasonable that they should be there and that the Spaniards might justly think ill of it. The Duke always after that observed the same circumspection when he wished the officers of the French army to enter into conversation with him.[1]

The French had immediately set to work constructing their siege lines on the approaches to Mardyke:

> The forage in the neighbourhood having been eaten up, they were obliged next morning to go and look for some on three great farms which were at only a half cannon shot from the Spanish trenches. These had been preserved through the influence the owners had with relatives who were officers of the Spanish army. There was even a regular guard to prevent anyone touching them. The commander of this guard, when he saw the French approaching with horse and foot, could not but judge for what purpose they were coming. But, following the laudable custom of the Spaniards, he drew back without daring to fire the farms, because he had received no order to do so.
>
> The cannon in the Spanish lines opened fire when the vanguard of the enemy approached. The Duke of York, whose quarters were only half a mile from there, galloped up and found that the French were already working to get cover and

---

[1] Sells, *Memoirs of James II*, pp.239–40.

entrench themselves so as to defend themselves in case of attack. Meeting the Prince de Ligne who was that day filling the office of *maestre de campo general*, the Duke asked him what he intended to do and whether he wished to let the enemy forage quietly in front of his eyes. The Prince replied in his usual way, that without the orders of the Marquess of Caracena or of Don Juan, he durst undertake nothing. Thereupon the Duke answered that before they could arrive, the French would be entrenched and it would no longer be possible to dislodge them or to burn the forage. The other responded that that was true, but he would undertake nothing without positive orders. The Duke told him that he was himself going to attack the enemy with his own troops and asked the Prince only to draw up his infantry along the line. But the other replied that, the bridge being in the Spanish quarter, he could not permit him to pass that way, because if there was anything to be done it was for the Spaniards to do it. Thus all these proposals served no purpose, and while orders were awaited from Dunkirk, the French foraged without being disturbed by anything but the cannon which kept firing on them. The noise brought the Prince de Conde from Bergues. The Duke of York informed him of what had passed between himself and the Prince de Ligne. The Prince de Conde was not at all surprised, and assured the Duke that when he had served with the Spaniards as long as he, the Prince, had, he would get accustomed to seeing them commit many great faults without being astonished. The enemy having foraged as long as they pleased drew back, leaving behind them about one hundred horses that the cannon had killed. It is not known how many men they lost, but no dead bodies were found, whether because they had taken them away or because they had buried them on the spot in some place which could not be discovered.[2]

Mardyke surrendered two or three days later. Ten guns, 400 soldiers, and a large number of officers, many of them officers, were captured. The next day the fort was handed over to the English, the French leaving after repairing the breaches in the defences and filling in their siege trenches.

Cromwell hoped that Turenne would now move against Dunkirk, and offered another 5,000 regulars if the French would agree to begin operations. However, Turenne decided to make Gravelines his next objective. It was thought to be weakly garrisoned and poorly supplied, but on the approach of the French the Spanish garrison opened the dykes and flooded the surrounding countryside. Turenne pulled back to Ruminghem, on the left bank of the River Aa, between St Omer and Ardres.

A garrison of 800 English troops was placed in Mardyke and a mixed force of 2,000 at Bourbourg. The English contingent was now split in three: three battalions in Mardyke, three in Bourbourg, and six with the field army. The English troops at Mardyke were soon encountering problems. The main fort would hold no more than 500–600 men, and the English plan was to rebuild and extend the fortifications so that they would hold a garrison of 2,000 horse and foot. Turenne agreed to remain in supporting distance with the bulk of the army for ten days until the work was completed.

---

2 *Ibid.*, pp.241–2.

Mardyke.

It was reported on 6 October that Mardyke 'may be sufficiently maintained against a storm or sudden surprise, but may easily be gained by one week's approaches.'[3] The old defences needed to be reinforced with three bulwarks. This would provide accommodation for 2,000 foot, which would be enough to safeguard Mardyke during the winter, though it would be 'a work of great difficulty' to prepare lodgings and carry out the repairs because of the lack of timber in the area.[4]

It had been intended that the allies should next besiege Gravelines, but the Spanish frustrated this by flooding the surrounding area, and also caused plans to quarter part of the English force near Calais to be abandoned. The troops must return to Mardyke, for 'as bad as the weather is, we cannot march one half day without a great loss of our men.'[5] There was discontent that the allies had not followed up the capture of Mardyke by opening the siege of Dunkirk. Vice Admiral Godson with the English naval squadron commented wryly to General Monck: 'our French file leaders have marched the wrong way to get Dunkirk this year.'[6]

The Duke of York related that:

---

3 Firth, *The Clarke Papers*, vol. III, p.176.
4 *Ibid.*
5 Birch, *Thurloe State Papers*, vol. vi, p.561.
6 Firth, *The Clarke Papers*, vol. III, p.189.

The Spanish continued in camp where they were, and it was announced that they would retake Mardyke. The sickness caused by the unhealthful air was so general that, except for the native-born Spaniards, few officers and soldiers escaped fevers, and more than half were at one and the same time incapable of doing duty. The troops commanded by the Duke of York suffered the worst; he himself was almost the only person among the officers or volunteers of quality, or the members of his household, who was not attacked. The Duke of Gloucester left the army, sick, and the Prince of Conde was holden with such a fever that the doctors feared for his life.

Soon after this the King of England came to Dunkirk to solicit Don Juan concerning some private business, and to remind him of some promises which he had made his Majesty in relation to England.

The English in Mardyke started repairing the old fortifications around that fortress, work which was all the more easy as the ditches had not been filled in and only a small part of the parapet had been levelled. Don Juan being warned of this resolved to march there one night with the whole army in order to destroy in the space of a night the defence works which they had been building for a month. This was more out of ostentation and to make his men believe that he designed to retake the fort, than from any hope of success.[7]

On 14 October an agent informed John Thurloe:

There is fresh intelligence that the enemy have effected all their preparations in order to the storm of Mardyke, and intend putting it into execution within two nights. If they do, they will be very honourably received, for there is very considerable strength in the fort and many of them men of much gallantry. It is my opinion that 20,000 will but fool themselves to make an attempt, judging it a matter of extraordinary difficulty to gain that place except they be so much masters of the field as to make their approaches by degrees, so as to force the shipping out of the Splinter, and hinder the constant supply of victuals.[8]

The Spanish and Royalist force consisted of between four and five thousand men.

The day having been appointed for this expedition, he [Don Juan] marched out of Dunkirk at the head of the army and accompanied by the King of England. The darkness was so great that they had to proceed by torchlight; which, when the enemy perceived, they thought the Spaniards were going to storm the place or at the least lay siege to it, and they prepared to defend themselves by lighting torches round the fort. When the army arrived within rather less than cannon shot, they extinguished their torches. His Majesty, Don Juan, and the Marquess of Caracena then halted with the cavalry, while the infantry was advancing. The Spaniards, marched to that part of the outworks that looked towards Dunkirk, the Comte de

---

7   Sells, *Memoirs of James II*, pp.242–3.
8   Birch, *Thurloe State Papers*, vol. vi, p.630.

Marsin with the Prince de Conde's foot, to the part that looks towards Gravelines; and the Duke of York, at the head of his troops, posted himself between the two.

When they approached the fort, the enemy kept up a continual fire of cannon and musketry, and the little frigates that were in the canal did not cease firing either. The infantry suffered very little because they got straight into the shelter of the old outworks; but the balls which passed over their heads fell among the cavalry and killed men and horses. His Majesty having gone forward to see what the infantry were doing, the Duke of Ormonde who was with him had his horse killed under him by a cannon shot. Each corps, on arriving at its position, sent its workmen forward with soldiers to support them. But the ditch was too deep in the Duke of York's position and he was obliged to send them round to where the Spaniards were to attack. In the meantime he had the ditch filled with fascines, and caused a passage over to be made so that he could support them if the enemy made a sortie.

While the workmen were beginning to raze the fortifications, the soldiers who had been detached in support kept up a continual fire on the enemy, and continued to do this until early dawn, when, the outworks being razed, the army drew off in good order and arrived at Dunkirk where it was beginning to be broad daylight.

The enemy were surely more surprised by the retreat than the attack, and they so little expected the Spaniards to retire so soon that they were still firing when the troops had been gone a good half-hour. There were not more than twenty horsemen, a captain of Gloucester's regiment and three or four soldiers killed; there were eight or ten wounded. The English in the fort, as was learned since, had only one man killed. And they believed so firmly that they would be besieged, that they despatched a messenger to monsieur de Turenne to warn him of it. He assembled his troops who were in forage quarters and began to march to their help; but, on being advised that the Spaniards had drawn off, he returned to his quarters.[9]

The English Royalist leadership were concerned by the way King Charles had been so close to the hottest action, and Edward Hyde wrote to him: 'I am none of those who think that you are like to recover your three kingdoms without being in danger of your life, but let it be when the adventure is of use and there is a recompense in view. Truly Sir, you ought to take some compassion of us.' The upshot was that the King henceforward left military command and involvement to the Duke of York.[10]

A few days after this an attempt was made to seize the English frigates which were lying in the canal:

> The first design had been to burn them, but this being judged too difficult, it was resolved to try and surprise the two larger ones, the "Rose" and the "True Love", which mounted six or eight cannon each. For this action twelve shallops were armed and sent out in very calm weather. Don Juan warned the King and the

---

9 Sells, *Memoirs of James II*, pp.243–4.
10 Firth, *The Clarke Papers*, vol. III, p.1155.

'BETTER BEGGING THAN FIGHTING'

Duke of York and they went along the shore accompanied by all the persons of quality and the principal officers to see what success the enterprise would meet with. There was a kind of mist. When they came over against the frigates, an English seaman was heard calling out "What ship's boat is that?", and on no one's replying, this man, seeing another shallop that was going to board the frigate, raised the alarm and fired a cannon shot which broke the leg of one of the rowers. This accident and a few musket balls that were fired at the same time terrified the shallops which drew off shamefully without attempting anything further.[11]

An English account of the attack gives further details:

Charles Stuart came three nights ago to Dunkirk, and on Saturday at night Don Juan sent out 700 horse to alarm Mardyke and manned a great many boats and a fireship with resolution to fire our shipping that were within the Splinter, but one of our frigates perceiving their design, discharged several guns among them, which forced them back (four considerable persons being slain) most of them which came by sea were drunk, but such as came by land frighted our men so much that they quitted the counterscarp and retreated to the fosse border very unworthily which is a great trouble to us. The fault must be in some officers, for where they stand, the soldiers never flee. We have abundance of sick men and are likely to be more, for sickness here is very rife. It takes them with giddiness in the head, and distracts, many swellings in the legs and joints, violent fever, and agues of all sorts. Several die daily by reason of ill accommodation and the slight care the French take of us.[12]

On 4 November Lieutenant Colonel Richard Hughes reported 'the sick of all the army are a very sad sight to behold; the Lord comfort them, for we have neither firing, straw or covering save what we pay for.' However he felt that the recent repulse of the enemy attack had done something to improve morale: 'Our soldiers hath gained their old courage, and stand stoutly to their work, for the enemy approached towards our works about 10 at night, and lodged themselves very near the same for six hours, but were very gallantly repulsed, forced to withdraw before day, leaving their faggots, spades, and pick axes, with some hand granadoes behind them.' But he added that seven or eight men a day were dying in Mardyke. 'We have three Colonels very sick, with abundance of officers and above 1,000 soldiers.' The sickness was probably typhoid, which also ravaged the French and Spanish armies.[13]

The fort was of course badly overcrowded, though as engineer Joachim Hane reported from the garrison on 5 November: 'the safety of Mardyke doth chiefly consist in the strength and number of men.'[14]

There were a number of problems, as Hane recounted in more detail on 30 November. There was a serious lack of timber to build huts, with only enough of them for 600 out of 2,000 men, the remainder having to seek what

---

11 Sells, *Memoirs of James II*, p.244.
12 Firth, *The Clarke Papers*, vol. III, p.25.
13 *Ibid.*
14 Birch, *Thurloe State Papers*, vol. vi, p.648.

shelter they could in tents: 'Besides empty promises we have got but little hitherto, which neglect makes the condition of the soldiers very miserable, and so destructive that [each day] we send no less than 10, 12 and more to the grave. The shifts we make for lodging are very hard and unwholesome, leading to the destruction of many every day.'[15] Their opponents fared little better. The Duke of York, quartered at Dunkirk, claimed never to have more than a quarter of his men fit for duty.[16]

The first Physician General of the English forces in Flanders was Doctor John French, but he may well have been a victim of the sickness widespread among the English troops, as he died at Boulogne in October 1657. He was succeeded by Doctor Saltonhall who received a £50 advance in pay, possibly as an inducement.

Medical supplies consisted almost entirely of the stock held by individual regiments, for the intention was that all except those with minor injuries or sickness should be brought back to England for treatment. There was however little consideration given to their reception when they arrived there, and many of the more lightly injured deserted to the Royalists in hope of receiving better care. One group stole Sir John Reynolds' treasure chest and took it with them. As the number of sick increased, many were sent to the French military hospital at St Quentin. However during the winter the highest rates of sickness were among the English troops serving with the French army, whose needs were almost totally neglected by the French.

For those brought back to England, their care in local communities, usually the coastal towns where they were landed, was supposedly paid for by the Commission for Sick and Wounded Seamen, with a payment of 7*s.* per week for each man. In practice, the authorities in ports such as Harwich and Dover would complain of considerable difficulty in obtaining these payments. Robert Jones, a surgeon at Harwich, on 11 February 1658 petitioned for a payment of £202 11*s.* to cover the cost of caring for 125 sick soldiers from Mardyke. He was fortunate, for on 25 March he received a payment of £261 10*s.* from the Navy Treasurers. Other carers were never paid. The battle of the Dunes resulted in increased demands for care of those wounded there. Though the official version of casualties admitted to only 40 dead and 20 wounded, on 17 June Sir William Lockhart reported to Thurloe plans to cater for 600–700, including 300 battle casualties.[17]

Some of these may have been incurred during the siege of Dunkirk, and after the town fell some casualties and sick were quartered in a house adjacent to a nunnery. The nuns were paid one styver a day for each man they cared for, providing warm broth, bread, meat and beer and clean linen. In theory one nun would care for up to eight soldiers, who were each paid half the standard rate. The care system, swamped by casualties from the battle and siege, broke down by the end of June, possibly worsened by religious differences between the nuns and their charges.

---

15 Firth, *The Clarke Papers*, vol. III, p.48.
16 Sells, *Memoirs of James II*, p.242.
17 Birch, *Thurloe State Papers*, vol. vi, p.69.

'BETTER BEGGING THAN FIGHTING'

The Savoy Hospital, London.

In an attempt to cope better, eight hospitals, one for each regiment, were opened in Dunkirk. They were to be staffed by 'a convenient number of women' who might be from the town or Flemish. Medical supplies were paid for by the Council of State. Gradually patients were repatriated to England, and a reception centre set up in Dover, staffed by surgeon Edward Cooke and a surgeon's mate. Cooke was granted £200 to cover his costs, but problems quickly arose. Soldiers brought with them disease, especially typhus, which took its toll amongst the townspeople. Those who died included the Mayor, whose wife later appealed to the Council of State for financial help, saying that her husband had visited the sick and helped organise quarters for them. He had also 'endured the most noisome scents and smells'. He had hired servants to take care of the sick, and had encouraged the townspeople to quarter them, 'though they brought sickness and death into almost every family where they are.' Elizabeth Smith, the Mayor's widow, was left with six small children to support. There was some criticism of Dr Cooke's care of the sick and wounded, and possibly as a result of this, on 2 September a petition of the sick and wounded soldiers in Dover was sent to the Council of State:

> We have been carefully attended to by Edward Cooke, and his assistant, and our dangerous wounds dressed, but we know fractured bones may ossicles, may exfoliate in this cold piercing us, we beg removal to hospitals in London for further cure. We understand you have ordered the Dover surgeon to take care of us, but one is a public drunkard and the other too old for employment. We beg consideration, having ventured our limbs against the enemy.

There were 34 signatures and six marks for signatories;[18] the petition was referred to the commissioner for the Savoy and hospitals.

---

18 Eric Gruber von Arni, *Justice to the Maimed Soldier: nursing, medical care and welfare for sick and wounded soldiers and their families during the English Civil Wars and Interregnum, 1642–1660* (Aldershot: Ashgate, 2001), p.139.

On the same day, possibly scenting criticism, Edward Cook and his fellow surgeons Robert Mustin, Daniel Stoker, and Guy Noble also petitioned the Protector and Council, asking 'not to be cast off in disgrace, having taken care of the sick and wounded, with not deserved calumny, nor reproaches. Some of the men are cured, and sent back to Flanders and others are fit to come to London.' Other sick and wounded were quartered in a small hospital in Deal, though many were sent to the military hospital in London, which they preferred.

One result of the Mardyke affair was increased friction between the French and English governments. Turenne had marched 'with incredible speed' to the support of the garrison when he learned of the Spanish approach, and arrived at daybreak next morning. He felt that Mardyke was too isolated and vulnerable to be held once the French army had withdrawn into winter quarters. He suggested that the defences should be demolished and Mardyke evacuated. The English leadership were incensed at the suggestion. It was seen as another example French perfidy, and Lockhart and Mazarin had heated exchanges on the subject. Cromwell warned the French ambassador that if he was compelled by Turenne's attitude to evacuate Mardyke the alliance would be at an end. This resulted in Turenne's advice being rejected, but Cromwell also demanded that the French should bear the costs of the English troops until such time that Dunkirk was captured, saying that both were actually by the treaty to be handed over to England at the same time, and until then the maintenance of Mardyke and its English garrison should be at French expense and should until then be under the command of a senior French officer.

Unsurprisingly, Mazarin rejected this view, but mutual distrust remained between the allies. Mazarin protested 'that except there were mutual confidence between persons that pursued a joint interest, their common undertakings would never have good success.'[19]

In the end a compromise was reached. Reynolds was commissioned by Louis XIV as Governor of Mardyke. Mazarin promised French support in holding Mardyke and the neighbouring outpost of Bourbourg, and financial assistance and military engineers were provided for the completion of the defences. As a pledge of French sincerity the garrisons were reinforced by eight of the Garde Française and eighty of the Cardinal's Guard, along with a number of French officers as volunteers.

When Turenne eventually went into winter quarters, he agreed to leave 300 horse at Mardyke, and stationed some of his best units, including the French and Swiss guard regiments, around Calais and Boulogne, within a day's march of Mardyke if the garrison came under attack.

Even so, the garrison was not regarded as secure. Work on the defences advanced slowly, according to the French because of the laziness of the English soldiers. It was a failing noted elsewhere by English commanders. The men were notoriously unwilling to dig, even in situations where attack

---

19 Jules Bourelly, *Cromwell et Mazarin; Deux Campagnes de Turenne en Flandre; la bataille des Dunes* (Paris: Perrin et cie, 1886), p.19.

was imminent. One engineer remarked that the men were 'very lukewarm in the business and not very docile,'[20] while others, equipped with spades, quit their work and went off to the dunes to dig up rabbits.

The English government blamed the situation at Mardyke on the French, who they claimed were failing to provide agreed supplies. Thurloe wrote that if Mazarin 'do not give some effectual order for supplying their wants that they may live, I do not see what other course can be taken but to call our men, home, which is much better than to have them die, or at least run away to the enemy.'[21] There were similar problems at Bourbourg and various French outposts.

Around the middle of November Turenne went into winter quarters around Guisnes and in Northern France. Three of the English regiments went with the French but continued to suffer heavily from the effects of disease. Early in January 1658 General D'Ormesson told Ambassador Bordeaux in London that he had sent the English soldiers who had been at Guines to join the Mardyke garrison:

> In regard his Eminence hath charged me in all his letters to take special care of them. I have done what lay in my power to accommodate them with all things necessary. These troops were conducted by very few officers and they seemed to me very feeble. I cannot impute this diminution to anything else but their officers, who are most of them absent, and the rest took no care at all of their sick men. I know they were well looked unto in their quarters, which were good ones, and exactly paid; whilst the French soldiers were forced to camp in huts and without any pay.[22]

It seems that the English officers followed the time-honoured custom of claiming pay for non-existent soldiers. D'Ormesson said that many of the companies were at only half-strength, but that the officers objected to him following instructions only to issue pay for those actually present. The officers responded by refusing to muster their companies, saying that 'some soldiers died at the end of the month to whom they had advanced pay for their subsistence, and that so this diminution would fall to their loss.' Mazarin complained to Lockhart about the 'unreasonable' English muster rolls, and that when his commissaries attempted to make actual musters, they were threatened with mutiny and desertions.[23]

In an attempt to regularise the situation, in January 1658 Turenne demanded that the six English regiments be reduced into four. He said that there now only 4,000 men left, which matched the establishment of four regiments:

> There is wanting of officers, who are either dead or have absented themselves without leave, to the number of eighty or ninety. Some of the officers who are

---

20 *Ibid.*, p.21.
21 *Ibid.*, p.23.
22 Birch, *Thurloe State Papers*, vol. vi, p.651.
23 *Ibid.*, p.652.

present are not so fit for their commands as were to be wished, who by this reducement might be purged out, and the body restored to a better condition than formerly. And to the end he might clear himself from having intentions to save money, or infringe the treaty, he offered, that at the same time His Highness [Cromwell] shall assent to the aforesaid reducements he will give ready money for 2000 new men to be raised, and put into two new regiments with officers as His Highness shall think to give them, and added that the most essential motive that inclined him to desire this favour from his Highness was, that all the officers of that body might by this example be taught to expect their continuance in the future from the zeal they should express in keeping their companies complete; which he said will be no small advantage to the common interest; and blamed the officers for being very careless in this point heretofore.[24]

Some of the problems undoubtedly resulted from the hasty way in which the English regiments had been raised and organised, but as it was, the condition of Cromwell's men worsened with the onset of winter. By the end of the year only 3,000 men remained of the original 6,000, and of these a third were generally too sick for duty. In December Reynolds declared only about 1,000 foot were available to defend Mardyke, and there were no more than 1,800 men in total fit for action in France and Flanders. This was partly designed to persuade Turenne to send to Mardyke the English regiments quartered elsewhere.[25]

The French later estimated that 2,000 English troops died in Mardyke over the winter. But they claimed in November that there were 3,733 English troops – it is not clear if this included officers – still in France and Flanders. In December the French said the English part of the Mardyke garrison included 1,060 privates and NCOs, 36 dragoons and 52 officers, with 240 other men who were sick. The French were providing 307 soldiers and 38 officers.[26]

Turenne had already refused a previous request for the return of the other English troops, feeling that Mardyke was sufficiently garrisoned and that it was under no immediate threat. If such an attack appeared likely, he suggested that Cromwell keep 500 soldiers, drawn from some of the veteran troops of the standing army, permanently on board ships ready to reinforce Mardyke at short notice. The English authorities, with some justification, rejected this idea of a 'rapid reaction force'. Thurloe said that it was not possible to keep troops on permanent standby on board ship. He claimed that it was very difficult to find new recruits to fill out the ranks of the depleted existing units, mainly because of the poor treatment which English troops had received from the French. 'I think it almost as possible to persuade them to leap into the sea as to go to Flanders in the French king's service.' The most that Cromwell felt able to do was to station the regiments of Colonels Salmon and Gibbon at Dover and Yarmouth, where they could be embarked quickly in case of need.[27]

---

24 Sir Thomas Morgan, *Memoirs*, pp.1–2.
25 Birch, *Thurloe State Papers*, vol. vi, p.659.
26 von Arni, *Justice to the Maimed Soldier*, p.133.
27 Birch, *Thurloe State Papers*, vol. vi, p.660.

'BETTER BEGGING THAN FIGHTING'

Marshal D'Aumont (1632–1704).

Reynolds was not placated. He proposed that the 1,000 men he claimed to be sick in Mardyke be sent home and replaced by 500 fresh men. 'I have no hopes of finding another expedient for the preservation of our soldiers or the safety of this place.'[28]

These concerns were one of several reasons which made Reynolds decide to return to England to put his concerns in person. He also had personal affairs to settle. Others claimed later that Reynolds wished to clear his name after an alleged meeting with the Duke of York. James claimed that the meeting was by arrangement, but it seems to have been motivated more out of curiosity than for any deeper reason, though Reynolds supposedly sent gifts of wine and forbade the Frigates from firing at either the King or Duke if they were seen riding along the beach.

It is difficult to be certain what actually passed between the two. As the garrisons of Dunkirk and Mardyke were near to each other, meetings between officers from the two garrisons were not infrequent. We have seen how officers with Charles II's forces had amiable contact with comrades they had known during their service in France. It seems most likely that Reynolds was merely copying this practice, and had no deeper motive, despite James' later claim that Sir John had 'let fall some dark expressions.'[29]

However a number of the English officers at Mardyke suspected the worse, and it was said that one of them, Lieutenant Colonel Francis White, of Cromwell's Regiment of Foot, who was now Governor of Mardyke, boarded the same ship as Reynolds with the intention of reporting the meeting to Cromwell. The ship was too small to cope with the stormy conditions encountered, and was wrecked on Goodwin Sands. Sir John Reynolds, Colonel White, and a number of other officers were drowned.

Verdicts in England on Reynolds were mixed. His old commander, Henry Cromwell, grieved for the loss 'of that worthy person, Sir John Reynolds.' General Fleetwood, perhaps more enigmatically, saw it as 'a sad and sore rebuke from the Lord.' A French officer said Reynolds was 'a very gallant person, and well beloved in our army.' Others, however, continued to suspect what lay behind the meeting between Reynolds and James. In January Sir William Lockhart mused from Paris: 'It is given out by some of Charles Stuart's faction here, that something passed at that meeting that I know he could not be capable of, neither do I believe that any such meeting was.' As

---

28 *Ibid.*, p.672.
29 Sells, *Memoirs of James II*, pp.245–6.

James later included the incident in his memoirs, it seems unlikely to have been purely a piece of Royalist propaganda, but there is not enough evidence to come to any firm conclusion regarding intent.[30]

Immediately after Reynolds' death there were rumours of Spanish preparations for a renewed attack on Mardyke, and Cromwell's contingency plans were put into operation. Twelve companies of foot were ordered embarked and within two days 500 men of Colonel Gibbon's Regiment reached Mardyke. The redoubtable Major General Morgan was appointed Governor. Mazarin sent a senior officer, Marshal D'Aumont, to supervise continued work on the defences, and some Swiss troops were sent to replace the French troops currently in the garrison.

There were now 2,500 troops in Mardyke, more than it could comfortably hold, and Lockhart was more concerned about the dangers of treachery from within than attack from without. Morgan reported Lockhart's view in December that before Colonel Gibbon's men arrived 'they had 1400 of the English foot that served all this campaign, 300 French foot, 200 officers, and 250 horse, which can be no inconsiderable garrison for such a place.' Lockhart felt that Gibbon's men could safely be returned to England, and this was done in January, though the garrison was joined by the troops from Guisnes who had been quartered with the French. However Turenne remarked again on the poor quality of their officers:

> The troops sent from Guisnes were conducted by too few officers and they seemed to me very feeble. I cannot impute this diminution to anything else but their officers, who are most of them absent, and the rest took no care at all of their sick men. I know they were well lodged in their quarters, which were good and ones, and exactly paid. Whilst the French soldiers were forced to camp in huts and without any pay.[31]

Morgan wrote of his command: 'There was hardly a week wherein Major General Morgan had not two or three Alarms by the Spanish Army. He answered to them all, and never went out of his clothes all winter, except to change his shirt.'[32]

Lockhart was undoubtedly correct in his opinion, for although it was never fully utilised, English naval command of the approaches to the North Sea and English Channel was virtually unchallenged, and safeguarded the garrison. Not only could Mardyke be kept supplied, but the Spanish privateers were effectively bottled up in Dunkirk and Gravelines, and the Spaniards found it almost impossible to supply their garrisons by sea. A squadron under Vice-Admiral William Godson was stationed off Mardyke, and seamen sent ashore to work on the defences. Naval gunfire helped repel the Spanish attack on 1 November.

---

30 Birch, *Thurloe State Papers*, vol. vi, 6c65, 67v6, 680, 686, 733.
31 Sells, *Memoirs of James II*, p.240.
32 *Ibid.*, p.241

But the main value of the fleet lay in keeping the Mardyke garrison supplied. Virtually all of Mardyke's needs had to be supplied by sea, as the land route was liable to interception by the Spanish. Timber, food, fodder for horses, munitions, were all transported by sea from England.

Whilst the English squadron made it virtually impossible for the enemy to mount a siege of Mardyke, their presence could be interrupted by bad weather. In January 1658, the English ships were forced off station by 'a sharp and violent north-east wind [and] the continual flowing in of the ice which comes from the eastward.' Some smaller ships were iced into the Splinter, and the garrison had to break the ice on the moats of their defences twice a day. The Spanish army had gone into winter quarters at the end of December, though there was concern that they and the Royalists might try to take advantage of the absence of the English squadron to attempt a landing on the English coast, in co-operation with a Royalist rising. Mazarin's agents reported that the Spaniards intended to land Charles with 3,000 foot and 1,000 horse of his army at the end of January or early in February, bringing with them arms for 12,000 men. Although a few weeks later he was more optimistic, saying that the enemy had intended to take Mardyke first, and then embark at Dunkirk, 'but there now being little hopes of their carrying Mardyke, he believed their disappointment in that would go near to break their whole design, for those of Flanders would be loath to part with any forces so long as that thorn stuck in their sides.'[33]

The Royalist army had been distracted during the autumn by various disputes. There had been a continuing trickle of recruits during the summer, mainly Irish from service with France, though Lockhart told Thurloe 'the Duke's Irishmen are no better than sheep in a lion's skin.' Ormonde told Hyde on 10 July that 'Irish soldiers come apace from La Ferte's army, but no more English since the 35 that came by Cambrai', and on the 14th admitted 'not above one hundred of the English have as yet come over from the French army, but many are expected.'[34]

In the meantime the Royalists, waiting restlessly for action, found that inactivity led to violence. Lord Newburgh was killed in a scuffle on 12 September; Lord Taaffe reported to the King that 'monsieur Corail' quartermaster general to the Duke of York, had attacked him with a cudgel. The miscreant was brought before the Duke of York, who at a Court Martial sentenced him: 'he shall, on his knees beg pardon of Lord Taaffe, presenting him with a stick to use as he pleases.'[35]

The English deserters were also causing some problems. On 13 September the Earl of Bristol told the King that he had spoken to Don Juan 'on the business of the English Regiment of Guards, upon occasion of the unwillingness of some of the English who have come over in a body to join the Irish.'[36] And on 2 October he told Ormonde: 'The business of the regiment of Guards is not yet settled. Great [discontent] caused by a report of Blague's being sent

---

33 *Ibid.*
34 Macray, *Calendar of the Clarendon State Papers*, vol. 3, item 984.
35 *Ibid.*, item 1086.
36 *Ibid.*, item 1098.

Plate A

1. Charles II (1630–1685), a portrait of 1653.

2. James, Duke of York (1633–1701).

Plate B

3. Sir William Lockhart of Lee (1621–1675).

4. Don Juan of Austria (1629–1679).

Plate C

5. Commonwealth infantry, 1658 campaign.

(*see colour plate commentaries for full caption*)

PLATE D

6. Royalist Musketeer.
(*see colour plate commentaries for full caption*)

Plate E

7. Royalist trooper or junior officer of horse in the Lifeguard of the Duke of York.
(*see colour plate commentaries for full caption*)

8. Buff coat.
Courtesy of Shropshire Museum Service
(*see colour plate commentaries for full caption*)

PLATE F

8. Flanders.

9. A contemporary map of Flanders.

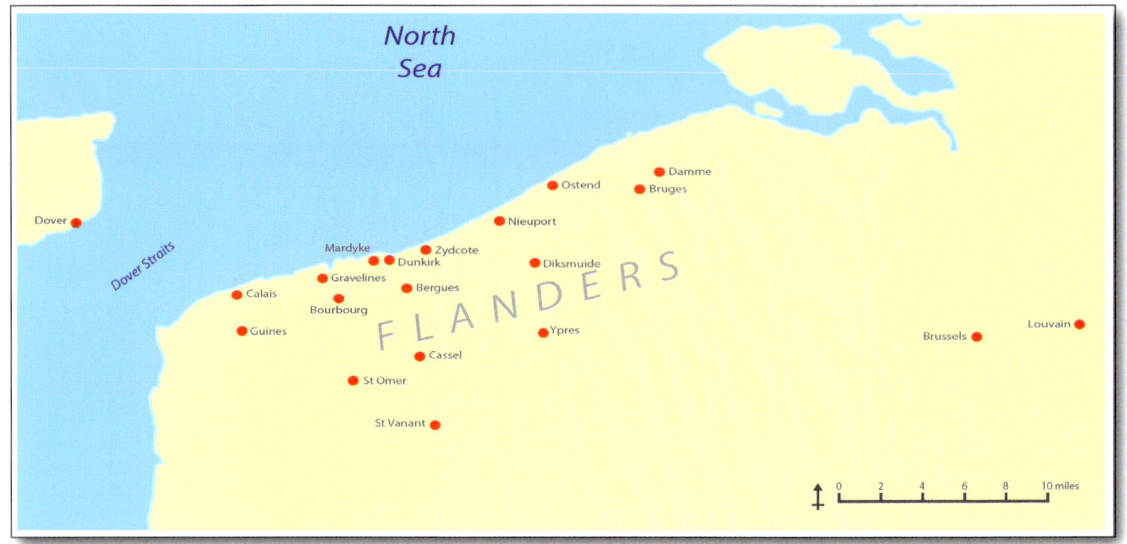

Plate G

10. The Siege of Dunkirk.

Plate H

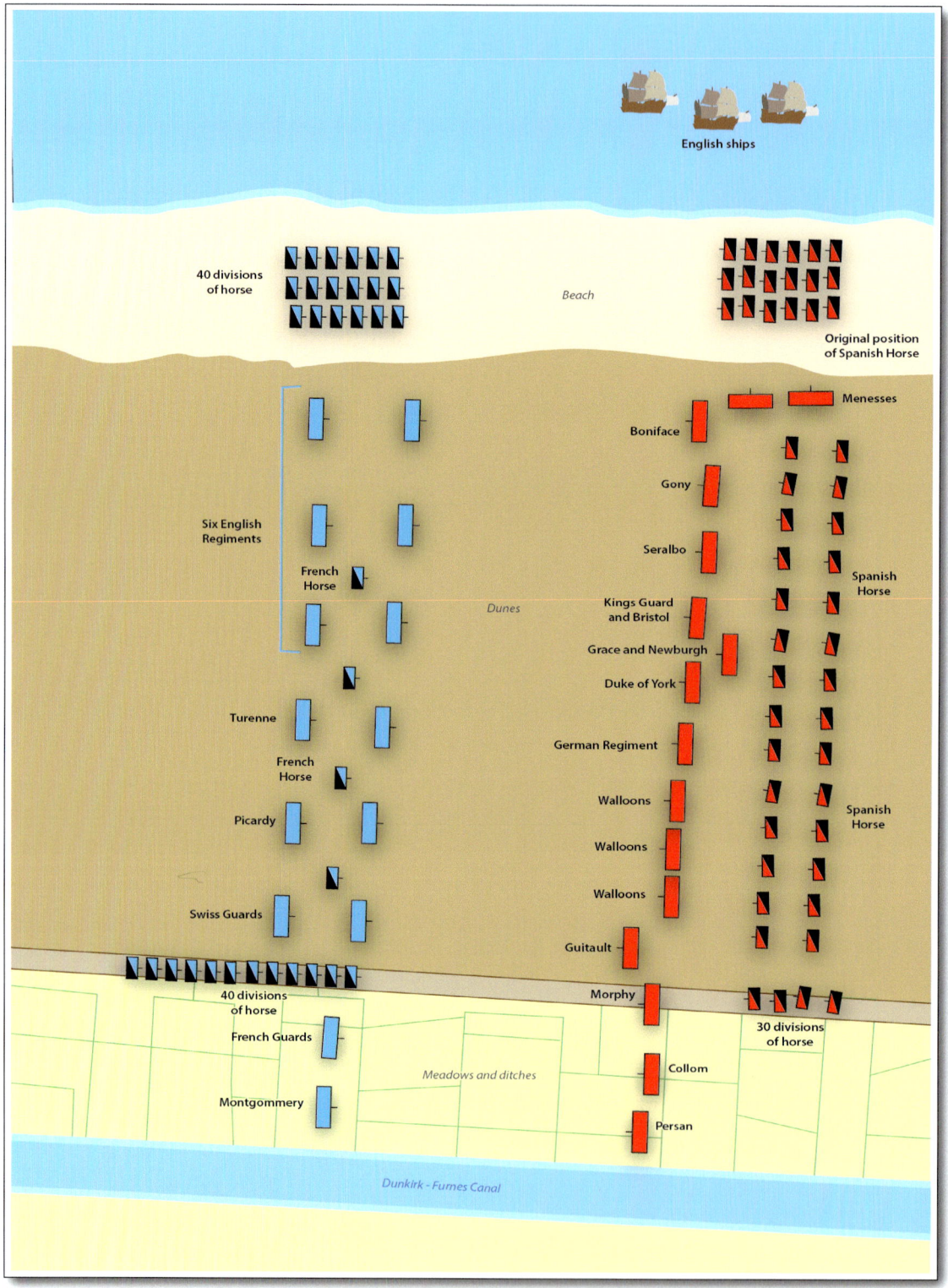

11. The Battle of the Dunes.

down to take care of that regiment, as Sir William Throckmorton [who had expected the command] has gone to Brussels in consequence. Sir William is a person of too much worth and merit to be disobliged by the preference of another before him.'[37]

Around the same time Hyde wrote to Bristol, saying that:

> The King especially commends to him the business of the Guards, upon which Colonel Blague comes to him. A good arrangement would have been made with the town at Dixmude had they not heard there of what had been done at Dunkirk. The King hopes Don Juan will declare the agreement at Dixmude void, otherwise he will be compelled to dismiss his guard with passes. Colonel Blague goes first to the Duke of York, to inform him, that under this agreement the men, instead of having lodging, board and two stivers a day, will only have two stivers. The King hopes Don Juan will be sensible of the villainy of the town in the murder of five soldiers.[38]

The end of the campaigning season left many soldiers ill-clad and unprepared for winter. On 5 November Hyde wrote to the King on the 'necessity of finding some means for clothing the naked soldiers.'[39]

The Royalist troops evidently suffered from sickness almost as much as their English enemies. James wrote:

> Few of the officers or soldiers, excepting only the natural Spaniards, escaped agues. Insomuch that we had never half our men together in a condition of doing duty. It fell most severely on those troops I commanded, for excepting myself, there was scarcely any officer or volunteer of quality, or any of my servants, who were free from an ague. My brother the Duke of Gloucester went out of the army sick of that distemper.[40]

However the absence of the English squadron allowed Spanish privateers to operate out of Gravelines, and made it possible to embark troops at Ostend.

King Charles returned to Brussels, but the Duke remained for some days at Dunkirk, as the Spanish appeared to be making preparations for a more regular siege of Mardyke. This seems to have been largely to keep the enemy unsettled, and on New Year's Day the order was given to put the army into winter quarters, and the Duke and the senior Spanish commanders returned to Brussels.

---

37 *Ibid.*, item 1116.
38 *Ibid.*, item 1152.
39 *Ibid.*, item 1155.
40 Sells, *Memoirs of James II*, p.242.

6

1658: The Campaign Begins

The renewal of the Anglo-French alliance, which it had been agreed should take place annually, seemed by no means a foregone conclusion. Lockhart had been reminding the government in England of this since early January, and by 16 February he was becoming anxious, telling John Thurloe: 'They [the French] suspect we delay bringing things to a conclusion upon some designs, that I believe his Highness [Cromwell] is far enough from thinking on; nevertheless his eminence [Mazarin] is very patient, though desirous that no more time is lost.'[1] Thurloe's response was cautious: 'They [the French] must declare their intention as to what they resolve to do this spring, and by what means and in what manner they intend to endeavour.'[2] Cromwell had been disappointed by the results of the previous year's campaign, and was determined that the French should stick to their undertaking to lay siege to Dunkirk.

Mazarin was resolved that the alliance should not fail, and on 16 March he had a meeting with Lockhart. The basis of the renewed treaty was agreed quickly. The French would undertake to make the attack on Dunkirk, and 'shall not decline that enterprise upon any pretences whatsoever.'[3] There were one or two near-hitches, when the French negotiators claimed that Lockhart was overbearing, but the treaty was signed on 28 March. The key clauses stated that Dunkirk was to be besieged by land and sea between 20 April and 10 May, before any other operations were begun. The French army with its English contingent was to attack by land, the English navy by sea. The English fleet would also keep the land forces supplied. After Dunkirk fell, the English fleet would assist the French in operations against Gravelines.

Thurloe remained sceptical regarding French intentions:

> The performance of it shall be punctually observed this side. I wish the same be done on the other side We will hope well, and that they will not do as they did last summer, especially they being under penalty if they do not besiege the place;

---

1 Birch, *Thurloe State Papers*, vol. vi, p.713.
2 *Ibid.*, vol. vii, p.31.
3 *Ibid.*, p.24.

unless they intend to turn that to their own advantage, and argue that the treaty is fulfilled if they either do the thing or submit to the penalty.[4]

There were already problems involving the attitude of the French and English soldiers towards each other. On 21 April Lockhart reported that:

> The French complain much against the insolency of the English soldiers at Mardyke. In a late quarrel they have killed some of the French king's guards, and the actors are neither punished nor apprehended, as the captains of the guards allege, and have writ to Major-General Morgan upon it, and have fully held forth the evil consequences may follow upon it.

Morgan was unconcerned and according to Mazarin simply commented that it was 'the result of the hatred which the English have for the French.'[5]

Both sides now began to prepare to take the field. On 1 April Morgan, with 400 foot and 50 horse from Mardyke, reinforced by 400 French troops from Bourbourg, marched towards Gravelines where he blew up two forts which protected the sluices which could be used to flood the area around Bourbourg.

The most pressing concern was to rebuild the English contingent, which was now at no more than half of its original strength of 6,000 men. Since early in the year Mazarin had been urging Thurloe to reorganise the force, and to ensure that existing companies were brought up to strength and officers distributed properly among them. In March Lockhart added his voice to French demands, saying that 4,000 men were necessary. In April Mazarin sent funds for 3,000 recruits, but, probably because of the bad reports of conditions in Flanders, they were slow to come in. In mid-May around 2,500 recruits reached Flanders, mostly untrained. Somewhat reluctantly Cromwell agreed to provide another 1,000 more experienced troops and sent half each of the regiments of Colonels Salmon and Gibbon.

On 27 February a naval squadron under Vice Admiral Godson commenced the blockade of Ostend and secured an early success by capturing or destroying some Dutch vessels which had been hired by the Spanish to transport Charles II's troops to England. This meant that for the moment the threat of a landing was lifted. Thurloe noted: 'From Flanders I am certainly informed that all intentions of prosecuting their designs against England are wholly laid aside, and with Charles Stuart's consent that business is deferred until September next.'[6] By April it had been put back still further until December. The presence of the English squadron also frustrated plans to transport 1,500 Spanish infantry from San Sebastian in Spain to Flanders, a serious blow to Don Juan who was critically short of foot.

Nevertheless, operations on land did not commence well for the allies. Initial plans were thrown into confusion when the garrison of Hesdin in Artois revolted. The governor of the town died and his deputy, Balthazar

---

4   *Ibid.*
5   *Lettres de Mazarin*, III p.350.
6   Birch, *Thurloe State Papers*, vol. vii, p.82.

Charles de Moncy Marquis d'Hocquincourt (1599–1658).

Fargues, on learning that the post would not be granted to him, rebelled. Marshal d'Hocquincourt and his regiment, who were in the town, joined him, and went over to Condé. The French were understandably reluctant to leave Hesdin in enemy hands, but Lockhart refused to consider making its recovery a priority over the operations against Dunkirk, although to deceive the enemy it was given out that the allies would first march on Hesdin.

During the winter the Royalists were chiefly concerned with how to keep their forces together both for the renewed campaign and for the intended invasion of England. The Earl of Bristol suggested to the Duke of York that the Royalist forces should be combined with those of Condé, in order to put pressure on the Spanish to comply with their undertakings to recruit and support the Royalist troops. The Duke decided the wisest course was to do nothing.

The main concern in Brussels was with preparations for the coming campaign. All reports indicated that the allies would lay siege to some important town or fortress, but the Spanish lacked sufficient foot to garrison all the potential targets properly. King Charles urged the Spanish commanders to concentrate on Dunkirk, which all the reports he was receiving from his agents and Royalist supporters in England indicated would be the Allies' target. However, the Spanish leadership believed that this information had been 'planted' to draw their attention away from Cambrai or another of the inland towns. As a result they failed to adequately garrison or provision Dunkirk, instead concentrating their efforts on garrisons in Artois, such as St Omer, and the frontier fortresses in Hainault, and especially Cambrai. At Dunkirk they failed to complete two sconces which they had begun on the Bergue–Dunkirk Canal, intended to block the route along the dyke if the surrounding countryside was flooded.[7]

In May the allies suffered another setback. The French had been negotiating for some time with Colonel Sebastian Spindeler, an officer in the Ostend garrison who had offered to betray the town for a price. Mazarin regarded him as unreliable, and abandoned the scheme. However Marshal d'Aumont, governor of Calais, received a report of a revolt in Ostend, and on 14 May, after considerable delay, attempted to land there with 1,500 men from Mardyke. He had with him two Lorraine regiments, two companies of the Garde Française, some *mousquetaires du roi* and an English company. As arranged with the conspirators, white clothes had been hung from the ramparts to indicate that the landing could go ahead safely. While the

---

7   Sells, *Memoirs of James II*, p.252.

1658: THE CAMPAIGN BEGINS

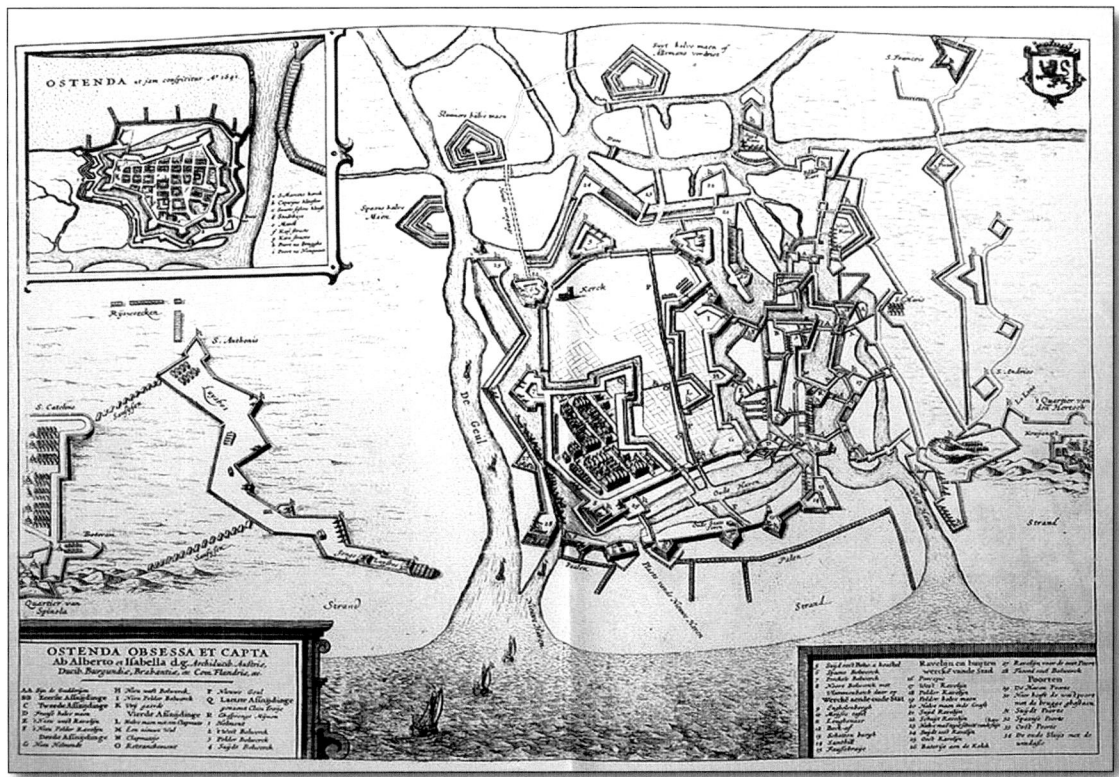

Ostend.

landing party assembled in nine boats, an agent was sent ahead to check the lie of the land. It appeared that most of the garrison had withdrawn, and the landing began. It was headed by D'Aumont himself with 100 English sailors Encouraged by an enemy officer who had apparently defected and who shouted 'Vive la France! Vive le Roi!' the advance party entered the town.

Suddenly large numbers of Spanish troops who had been concealed in nearby houses opened fire from all sides with cannon and muskets. The Spanish, having baited their trap, had reinforced the garrison with 3,000–4,000 more foot. Trapped and outnumbered, D'Aumont and his surviving men surrendered, and he and the men of the Garde Française and *mousquetaires du roi* who had been captured were paraded in triumph through Brussels. Lockhart observed sourly 'By all accounts, it is evident he hath fallen into a trap which he digged for himself.'[8] The English were uncharitably rather jubilant about the French reverse. Thurloe told Monck that Spindeler had made the same offer to Cromwell, who like Mazarin had rejected it. 'This we could have told the French had they pleased to have communicated it to us, but they managed it so privately that none but their enemies knew of their intentions.'[9]

Nonetheless, Turenne was ready to take the field. Early in May he assembled his army around Amiens, and crossed the River Somme on the

---

8   Birch, *Thurloe State Papers*, vol. vii, p.109.
9   *Ibid.*, p.103.

13th neat Corbie, and marched north-westwards, as if planning to attack Hesdin. There was a hope that the presence of Louis XIV with the army might persuade the rebel army to surrender. However Fargues had the town and garrison under firm control, and fired on the king and his escort. Turenne abandoned the attempt, and swung north-east, crossing the River Lys at Merville on the 20th, and reached Soex near Bergues three days later. During the march the French vanguard, consisting of Lieutenant General Francois de Blanchefort, with horse and 1,000 mounted infantry, surprised the enemy forces quartered at Cassel, capturing the Duke of Gloucester's regiment of 400 men, together with another Irish regiment serving with the Spanish. The Duke of York said that the fault lay with Monsieur de Bascourt, a *marshal de battaile* who was in command of the forces in that part of the country. Cassel, James felt, was indefensible. In the meantime the Duke of York's Regiment, 500 strong, with some other small units, was sent into St Omer, the Spanish commanders believing that town to be the French objective.[10]

By the time de Bascourt realised that Turenne's target was actually Dunkirk, it was too late for more than a few horse, led by de Bascourt himself, to reach it. De Leyde also only just managed to get back into the town.

By 21 May, despite several days of heavy rain which slowed his guns and supply wagons, Turenne reached Hazebrouck and halted for a day at Cassel to allow the laggards to catch up.

Turenne was now ten miles from Dunkirk, and ahead lay the most difficult part of the operation. As expected the Spanish had opened the sluices, flooding the approaches to Dunkirk. The only way of approaching the town was along the dykes running alongside the canal, and the Spanish had broken these down in places and had forts or sconces at others. Turenne repaired some of the gaps with planks and hurdles, or made his men wade waist deep through the floods. On the night of 24–25 May the French established themselves on the dyke of the Bergues–Dunkirk Canal, capturing two of the forts, including Fort Royal, and placing bridges across the canal. Other French troops under the Marquis de Castelnau had joined the English troops at Mardyke, and the combined force advanced along the west bank of the canal, linking up with Turenne on the 25th.

Lieutenant Colonel Richard Hughes marched with the Mardyke contingent, and reported that: 'Marshal Turenne came through Flanders as expected with 11,000 men, and gained the pass without opposition, and we on this side drew out 6,000 foot and 1,200 horse and forced our passage over two rivers and joined him.'[11]

Little had been done to strengthen the defences of Dunkirk since the siege of 1646, although the governor, the Marquis de Leyde, was a highly capable soldier. He had been Spanish ambassador to England in 1655, and had defended Dunkirk against Condé, then fighting on the side of the French crown, in 1645. He had around 2,200 foot and 708 horse. Dunkirk consisted of the Old and New Towns. The Old Town, with the harbour, was closest

---

10 Sells, *Memoirs of James II*, p.252.
11 Firth, *The Clarke Papers*, vol. III, p.131.

to the sea and was protected by the original stone town wall with towers at intervals. The outer defences of both the Old and New Towns consisted of a large earthen rampart and fosse, with a water-filled ditch 26 feet deep. The harbour was defended by the guns of Fort Leon, in the dunes to its northwest, and Fort de Bois at the end of the harbour, about 400 yards from the sea.

De Leyde had learned earlier that Turenne had planned to make Dunkirk his objective, and had gone in person to Brussels to beg for supplies and reinforcements. But his pleas went unheard. The high command in Brussels was convinced that Turenne intended Cambrai as his first objective, and that there was no immediate threat to Dunkirk. A frustrated de Leyde returned to Dunkirk, telling King Charles II that he was going to defend a town without men, ammunition or supplies against a superior enemy, and that all he could do was to lay down his life in its defence.

Spanish reaction to Turenne's march on Dunkirk was slow. The Duke of York complained of the Spanish commanders' reluctance to believe the intelligence they received until Turenne was well on his way:

> At which time, but no sooner, they ordered all the troops, which were in Nieuport, Dixmuyde and Furnes (of which they were jealous though without reason, because they were all English, Scots, and Irish) to march for Dunkirk, [retaining] only the King's Regiment of Foot, which was upwards of four hundred, and then lay at Dixmuyde, but these came too late, the Town being blocked up already. So that the Marquis de Leyde found himself besieged in a place, the main strength of which consisted in the outworks, which were very large, all of earth, and very easy to be approached. To all this great extent of ground which was to defend, his garrison was no ways answerable, for it consisted but of a thousand foot, and eight hundred horse, and his provisions of powder and other necessaries were very scanty, even with reference to the small number of his men.[12]

The Spaniards were critically short of infantry and of money – the latter partly a result of Blake's victory at Santa Cruz. This hindered both recruiting and the preparation of an adequate artillery train.

Turenne's combined force totalled around 25,000 men. Siege lines were opened on the south and east sides of Dunkirk, with headquarters among the dunes. Cavalry outposts were established in the direction of Zuydcoote to guard against interference from the enemy garrisons at Furnes and Nieuport. The English contingent, under Sir William Lockhart, with 2,000 French horse under Castelnau, were on the western side nearest to Mardyke. Four of the English regiments were stationed between the unfinished canal and the sea, the other two were interspersed amongst the French horse between the canal and Fort Royal.

Turenne's first task was to construct two lines of entrenchments: an interior one to maintain the siege against the garrison, and an exterior one to guard against attempts at relief or to bring in supplies. The line of approach along the beach was blocked with lines of stakes and chains.

---

12   Sells, *Memoirs of James II*, pp.253–4.

'BETTER BEGGING THAN FIGHTING'

Edward Montagu, later Earl of Sandwich (1625–1672).

Vice Admiral Godson was ordered on 24 May to leave two or three ships to blockade Gravelines and take the rest of his squadron to assist in operations against Dunkirk. He was joined on 4 June by General at Sea Edward Montagu, with the large ships of the squadron, bringing the total to over 20 ships. The squadron blocked Dunkirk and also bombarded its seaward defences. The presence of the fleet made it relatively easy to supply the besiegers with necessities first stored at Calais, then transported by sea to Mardyke. Mazarin took personal charge of organising supply and logistics, at an estimated cost of 10 million livres. Particular care was taken to provide for the wounded and sick. The French Queen Mother was asked by Mazarin to organise the care of those transported to Calais, and a field hospital was set up at Mardyke under Thomas de Grouchy as administrator.

For the first ten days of the siege the besiegers were fully occupied in constructing siegeworks, this made difficult by the sandy terrain and marshes. However on the night of 4 June active operations began. During the night Turenne made two attacks, on the right by troops including the Garde Française, and on the left by English foot. Each attack was supported by cavalry, and the operation was under the overall command of Lieutenant General de Varennes. At the same time that the allies began their attack, the Spanish made a sortie with 600 cavalry and some foot with the object of destroying the siege works. After some cavalry skirmishing the French gained the upper hand, and the Spaniards were pushed back to the counterscarp. In the English sector of the line, Lockhart's men at first retreated, but finally rallied.

On the morning of 5 June Fort de Bois, which had been coming under constant artillery fire, was evacuated by the Spanish.

On the evening of 5/6 June, French troops were relieving the Garde Française in the siege lines when approaching enemy troops were sighted. Turenne, who was close by, was urged to take cover when an officer was shot close to his side. There was concern about the marshal's safety on a number of occasions. Mazarin in a letter urged him to take care: 'In the name of God give the king that mark of zeal you have for his service, and to me in the friendship you have promised, and consider, I pray you, what will be if you are wounded.'[13]

On the night of 6 June the garrison made another sortie, with eight squadrons of horse from the Nieuport Gate. They attacked at two points one on part of the line held by the Garde Française. In a sharp cavalry contest

---

13 Sir Thomas Morgan, *Memoirs*, p.2.

the French repulsed their attackers, taking ten prisoners, including a cornet, who provided some details of the strength of the garrison.

The English were involved in repulsing some of these sorties. Lockhart reported of one:

> The action passeth for a handsome one in the report of the French, who are not over apt to flatter us. The enemy have been so well satisfied with the supper they then got they have not expressed any appetite for a breakfast or any other meal of that nature.' Lieutenant-Colonel Richard Hughes said: 'Our English soldiers behaving themselves very handsome, have gained a general applause from all the grandees of the army; the French horse, who formerly hated us, are becoming very loving and civil, and had rather engage with us than with their own.[14]

Although none of the engagements were major, repeated skirmishes caused English losses to mount steadily. It was said that they suffered fifty or sixty casualties every night. And losses from disease also continued. Hughes wrote:

> Our friends in England, have been very careless of us; the three thousand tents ordered us by the Council five weeks ago are not yet come, which causes a great sickness amongst us, having not one piece of wood within six miles to hut with… Our mortar pieces and shells have been here these three weeks, but the firemaster is still in England.[15]

On the night of 6 June French horse under the Marquis de Schomberg intercepted an enemy party taking letters from the Marquis de Caracena in Brussels to the Spanish garrisons at Linck, Burgues and Gravelines. He informed them that Don Juan was preparing to relieve Dunkirk, and called most of the regular troops and militia from these garrisons to join him. Spanish troops being concentrated between Ypres, Furnes, Diximude and Nieuport had already made enemy intentions clear to Turenne, and it was apparent that a Spanish move was imminent. He warned Mazarin that the enemy did not intend just a diversion, but would risk everything in an attempt to relieve Dunkirk. Mazarin promised infantry reinforcements but these would not in the event arrive in time for the battle. Neither, despite pleas, would Cromwell send any additional troops. Turenne constructed a number of redoubts on the contravallation of the siege lines in the dunes, and a battery of three guns, directing their fire at the Spanish-held Fort de Boige.

During the evening and night of 7 June a gale hindered construction work, and bad weather continued into the following afternoon; when, covered by the fire of 20 guns, six squadrons of horse and 300 foot sortied from Dunkirk and advanced along the beach, wrecking the trenches and barricades there. Taken by surprise, and disrupted by the gale still raging across the dunes, the

---

14 Birch, *Thurloe State Papers*, vol. vii, p.126.
15 Firth, *The Clarke Papers*, vol. III, p.138.

French fought back, though suffering some heavy losses. When the alarm was raised in the French camp, Turenne and a number of officers hastened to the scene of the fighting. Officers of all ranks, and volunteers, with or without the troops of their commands, engaged the enemy and bore the main brunt of repulsing the attack, with the rank and file suffering only light losses.

During the next few days operations seemed to be reaching a climax. The first task of the besiegers was to repair the damage suffered in the Spanish sortie, and then to commence an increasingly effective bombardment. The Spanish countered by throwing bombs and grenades into the defenders' forward trenches. Despite this, the siege works were steadily pushed forward. Artillery was positioned on the beach, and fired on two defending guns positioned on the jetty; two batteries were established in the dunes below Fort Leon.

7

The Battle of the Dunes

The Duke of York remembered that:

> The certain intelligence of this Siege [Dunkirk] being come to Brussels about the end of May, gave no small trouble to the Spaniards, especially when they saw all hopes of putting succours by sea were wholly vanished, by reason that the English Navy under the command of General Montagu were now come before it. So that the only prospect which they had of relieving it was by the Army. And therefore it was immediately resolved in a Council of War, (where were present all the General Officers) that the army should draw together at Ypres with all imaginable haste, pursuant to which, the orders were immediately dispatched for all their troops to meet at the Rendezvous.[1]

By 7 June between 12,000 and 14,000 Spanish and Royalist troops were at Ypres. The commanders decided to march to Furnes, and on the 9th reached Nieuport. The next day, between Odekerk and Furnes, the Spaniards were joined by Marshal d'Hocquincourt, who had hoped to raise a rebellion in the Vexin and Normandy, but, his plot discovered, was forced to flee to join the other Frondeurs under Condé.

On 11 June another Council of War was held; present were Don Juan, Caracena, Condé, d'Hocquincourt and de Ligne. The Duke of York was not there, but described what took place, based on the account of a participant who wished to clear himself from any responsibility for what had been decided:

> Don Juan informed them of the cause of their meeting. That it was to consult on the most proper method of relieving Dunkirk. He let them know the present condition of the place, which was such as required a speedy succour, and after having enlarged upon these heads, he proposed to them that the Army should march to Zudcote, and camping there amongst the sand hills, as near as they could to the Enemy's Lines, should watch their opportunity of attacking them. After this proposition, there was a long silence, and no one arising to oppose it,

---

1   Sells, *Memoirs of James II*, p.254.

he said: 'Since I see you all approve of what I have proposed, let us now consider after what manner, and what time, we shall march thither.' Upon which it was resolved they should all go the day following to view the ground for encampment, and observe the Line of the Besiegers.[2]

James would later criticise Caracena in particular for failing to speak against Don Juan's plan.

Turenne had learnt on the 10th of the Spanish march. The next day he ordered the construction of a large 'place d'armes' at the edge of the siege works at which troops could be assembled. He had 20 guns emplaced there to keep up a bombardment of the defences. The garrison responded with a sortie of six or seven squadrons of horse to investigate the siege lines, and from the other side 40 of Don Juan's Lifeguard made a probe to explore the nature of the barricade which Turenne had established on the beach.

French scouts reported the Spanish relief force to be in the area of l'Abbey des Dames near Furnes, two or three hours' march away; during the night of the 10th there was some skirmishing in the siege lines, with troops from the garrison throwing some grenades at the section of the lines held by the English troops, but without effect.

On June 12, the relief force mounted a major reconnaissance of the enemy positions. The Duke of York took part:

> We went on the 12th, with our four thousand horse, and the commanded foot, with intent to view the Enemy's Line, and choose the place for our encampment. Being advanced as far as Zudcote, we halted there, and first made choice of our ground to lodge the Army, before we went nearer to discover the Enemy. This was done by the Marquis of Caracena, Don Estevan de Gamarra, and myself, who taking some horse along with us, went across the Sandhills, till we came to the Strand. In the meantime Monsieur de Boutteville was gone with our Cravats along the highway betwixt the Sandhills, and the meadow ground, advancing towards the Enemies' horse guard so far, that he began to Skirmish with them, and forced them to give back a little, by which means he had the opportunity of coming within a convenient distance of their Lines, and viewing them.
>
> As he was returning to give the Generals an account of what he had observed, he met the Marshal d'Hoquincourt, who earnestly desired him to turn once more, saying he would charge the Enemy's Horse Guards; and not withstanding that Monsieur de Boutteville, used many arguments to dissuade him (as having already done what he intended, and brought back a prisoner or two with him, which he had taken amongst the Sand-hills) yet the Marshall remained obstinate, and over-persuaded him to go back, by which he did not only engage himself, but almost all of the rest of the General Officers at a great distance from their troops, for the Prince of Conde seeing him go that way, walked after him, and Don John, hearing the Prince was gone towards the Line, did the like. And last of all, I, having observed all that could be seen where the Marquis and I had been together, and coming that way, where I had heard that those whom I have already

---

2   *Ibid.*, pp.255–6.

mentioned were gone before, put on a large gallop after them, and came up to them, just as Monsieur d'Hocquincourt had forced the enemy's horse guards to retire. In performing which, Henry Jermyn on our side, and the Marquis de Blanquefort, at present Earl of Feversham, nephew to Monsieur de Turenne, on the other, were both of them shot through the thigh.

The Marshal d'Hocquincourt was now come within musket shot of a redoubt, which the Enemy had advanced upon a height, somewhat before their Lines; when at the very moment that I came up to him, he received a shot in the belly from the said redoubt, of which presently after he died. Upon this we drew off, the enemy at the same time beginning to advance upon us; and the Prince of Conde with his people, being very busy in taking the papers out of the Marshal's pockets, not knowing whether they should be able to bring off his body, a Gentleman who belonged to the said Marshal came to me and desired me to face about, to give them the leisure of bearing off his Master's Corpse, which at his request I did, and with some difficulty the body was brought away. But had the enemy pressed hard upon us, we had not only been forced to have left it behind, but all the General Officers there present had run the hazard of being made prisoners, they having no other horse with them besides Cravats, who were not capable of mounting a vigorous charge, and being distant from their own troops above a mile. But at length when all was over, up came the Marquis de Caracena with three troops of Guards to our assistance, who chid[ed] us all for exposing ourselves as we had done.

After this we returned to the body of our Army, but so disordered by the fatal accident which had happened to the Marshal d'Hocquincourt, that we marched back to our camp by Runes, without viewing any part of the Enemy's Line or taking any other consultation about our going thither.[3]

French reports added more detail concerning this skirmish. The Spanish reconnaissance party at about midday probed forward along the beach and through the fields bordering the Furnes Canal. The bulk of the 4,000 horse halted at Zuydcote to begin tracing the lines of the intended encampment. However the group of senior officers continued their reconnaissance and came upon a French cavalry outpost. As the Duke of York describes, a skirmish followed in which d'Hocquincourt 'with ardour more fit for a musketeer than a marshal' forced the enemy to give ground. At this point a party of 20 Swiss troops occupying an outpost in front of the main position opened fire, and d'Hocquincourt was mortally wounded. Other accounts say that he actually died an hour or so after being taken back to camp.

During the night the besiegers attempted to gain a foothold on the counterscarp of the Dunkirk defences, but were forced back by the defenders. At around the same time Turenne learnt from his scouts that the enemy were in occupation of some higher sand dunes as an advanced position from which they could observe the Anglo-French lines. Turenne ordered his entrenchment to be strengthened and artillery brought up. He also ordered the barrier across the beach to be improved.

---

3 *Ibid.*, pp.256–8.

Next morning the Spanish forces began a cautious advance. Their leading troops halted at 11:00 a.m., in a fold in the sand hills. As well as the dunes, the Spaniards also occupied on their left the fields by the canal. Their artillery and baggage had not yet come up.

On the French side, Turenne spent the morning checking his outposts, and seeing indications that the enemy were building a bridge of boats over the canal, concluded that they were definitely preparing to attack. On returning to camp he decided to pre-empt Don Juan by an advance of his own. He had initially found it difficult to believe that the whole Spanish field army was encamped so close to his position, but an escaped French prisoner was able to assure him that this was the case. Mazarin had also suggested that it would be better to seek battle with the enemy rather than await attack within the siege lines.

Turenne was aware that Condé had a good idea of the French position based on his own siege of Dunkirk in 1646, and that the enemy plan would be trap the French army between the relieving force and the garrison. Turenne's commanders readily agreed to his proposals, and a messenger was sent to inform Sir William Lockhart, who replied that he would confidently play his part in the attack.

There were in fact considerable differences between the accounts of Sir William Lockhart and Thomas Morgan regarding the events preceding the battle. Lockhart later wrote:

> One came to me from Mr Turenne, and told me there was a necessity of giving battle to the enemy tomorrow morning. I was much surprised with the shortness of the warning, and more with the strange providence was in it, for I had one of the most violent fits of the stone upon me, that I ever I had almost in my life, but finding there was no 'midds' [option] but either fighting or abandoning the siege, I chose rather to trust in God with the event of a battle, than to give over so hopeful a cause. And so about ten o'clock we drew out the forces, and put myself at their head in a coach, and reached Mr Turenne's quarters next morning by break of day.[4]

This at any rate was Lockhart's version of events. Major General Thomas Morgan gave a much more dramatic account, suggesting that it was only as a result of his persuasions that Turenne agreed to seek battle, a version which is generally viewed as being almost entirely fiction.

Lieutenant General Marsin, with three squadrons of horse and four regiments of foot would be left to guard the camp, while Lieutenant General Praedel with six squadrons of horse and 14 foot companies of the Garde Française would hold the left and centre of the siege works. The English left 1,000 foot to defend their section of the lines. The French baggage train was sent away to Fort Royal, the English to Mardyke.

Before dawn on 15 June the Allied army of 5,000–6,000 horse and 9,000–10,000 foot began its march. Turenne had snatched some sleep lying on the

---

4   Birch, *Thurloe State Papers*, vol. vii, p.127.

sand, wrapped in his cloak. A message arrived from his scouts that they had captured an enemy soldier, who reported that the Spanish had no artillery and that not all of their foot had yet arrived. It would be two or three days before Don Juan was ready to attack.

The Duke of York, meanwhile, according to his later version of events, was increasingly uneasy. He knew that the Spanish foot were short of powder. They were camped less than two cannon shot from the enemy, but:

Henry Jermyn (1605–1684).

> We took no measures in our army as if any Enemy were to be expected; for when the orders were given in our Camp at night, there was no prohibition made to our horse of going out to forage, till the pleasure of the General be further known, as is usual in the like cases. But they were permitted to go abroad, as if no Enemy had been near us. And, that it may be seen, how little some of our General Officers believed the French had any such intention (or at least would have it thought that they so believed) happening myself to be at supper that night with the Marquis de Caracena, and the Company falling into discourse on the subject of our coming thither, and what the French might probably attempt against us, I said that for my own particular I liked not our being there upon such terms as we were then, having no Lines nor any thing to cover us from the Enemy, and that it was my opinion, if they fell not upon us that very night, I was very confident they would give us battle the next morning. To which both the Marquis and Don Estevan de Gamarra answered that it was what they desired. To which I replied that I knew Monsieur de Turenne so well, as to assure them they should have that satisfaction.
>
> The next morning about five of the clock, our horse guard brought us intelligence, that they saw some horse drawing out of the Enemies' Lines, which they supposed came with design to beat them in; upon which our whole Army took the alarm, and stood to their arms, and the Generals went out to discover what the Enemy was doing. I was the first who came to our horse guard, and going as far as the outmost sentries, I plainly saw that their whole Army was coming out of their lines. Their horse, with four small field pieces, advancing along the highway betwixt the Sand hills and the meadow grounds, and the French foot drawing out on their left hand, having thrown down dome Pieces of their Line, that they might march out with at least a Battalion a front. And further on their left hand, which was nearer to the sea, the English were drawing out, whom I easily knew by their red coats. Of all which having taken a distant view, I went back to give an account of it, and before I reached our Camp, I met with Don Juan, who asking me, what were the intentions of the French? I answered him, that they were drawing out to give us battle. Which he, seeming not to believe, said, their design was only to drive in our horse guards. I replied that it was not the custom of the French to march out with such a body of foot, as I had seen, composed of the French and Swiss Guards, the Regiments of Picardy and Turenne, all of which

I knew by their colours, as well as the English by their red coats, and so great a body of horse as those I had observed with their cannon before them, with a bare intention of forcing in our horse guards.

Before I could add any other arguments for the confirmation of my opinion, or Don John had the leisure of replying, the Prince of Conde came up to us, who had also been at one of our horse guards, and gave the same account which I had done, and seeing the Duke of Gloucester there, he ask'd him, if he had ever seen a Battle? Who telling him he had not, the Prince assured him, that within half an hour he should behold one. And now, there being no further room to doubt of the Enemies' intentions, all the General Officers parted from each other, and went to their respective posts, with resolution to attend the coming of the French, and to fight them where we were, having the advantage of the ground, which we must have, lost had we advanced towards them.[5]

James, together with de Gomme's plan of the battle, gives details of the Spanish deployment. There were, they state, 6,000 foot, though it is unclear if this total includes officers. The foot were formed into 15 divisions, averaging in the region of 500 men or in some cases fewer, in each. Apart from two divisions, they formed one line from 'a high sandhill' near the beach to the meadows adjoining the Furnes Canal.

On the far right were the four regiments of 'natural Spaniards'. The Regiment of Don Gaspar Boniface was positioned on the high sand hill nearest to the beach. Posted behind Boniface and at right angles to him, facing the beach was the Regiment of Francisco de Menes, to guard against any attempt to outflank the Spanish army. To the left of Boniface was the Regiment of Don Diego de Goni, commanded by Don Antonio de Cordova, beyond this was the Regiment of the Marquis de Seralvo. Although De Gomme's plan may indicate that originally it had been intended to deploy some horse on the beach to the right of the Spanish foot in order to cover their flank, this did not happen. The Spanish regiments of Boniface and Gogua were thought to be in a sufficiently strong natural position to withstand any cavalry attack on their flank from the beach. The tide was in any case coming in, covering the beach, and any Spanish horse stationed there would have come under heavy fire from the English warships which were supporting the Allied army.

Then came Charles II's Royalists. Formed into one division were the two weak regiments of the Earl of Bristol and King Charles, led by Lord Muskerry. In reserve behind this division and also in one division, were the regiments of Richard Grace and the Scots of Lord Newburgh. The regiment of the Duke of York, the strongest of the Royalist units, was to the left of Muskerry. To their left were three Walloon regiments of the Army of Flanders, and after that a division made up of elements from four German regiments. Next, on the last sand hill before the meadows bordering the Furnes Canal were reached, the first of Condé's units, Guitard's German Regiment, was drawn up. Three other divisions of Condé's foot continued the line across the road and through the meadows to the canal.

---

5   Sells, *Memoirs of James II*, pp.258–60.

James felt that the foot occupied an excellent defensive position on the ridge of high ground, 'so that the Enemy must be constrained to charge us up the hill, which everyone knows is a greater disadvantage on the Sand, where the footing is loose, than on firm ordinary ground.'[6]

In theory the Spanish army had 8,000 horse, though James claimed that half were absent foraging. The Spanish horse were drawn up in two lines among the sand hills behind the Royalist foot, while Condé's horse were drawn up in several lines behind his foot, the enclosed nature of the ground in many places forcing them into a narrow frontage of three or four squadrons.

At 5:00 a.m. the Anglo-French army began its advance, part along the beach, a detachment along the Dunkirk–Furnes road and others through the meadows. The bulk of Turenne's troops crossed the dunes and formed up in a little open plain in front of the Spanish position. The difficult terrain they had to cross meant that the troops in the centre were not in position until 8:00 a.m.

Louis d'Humières (1628–94). A notable bon vivant, who dined off silver in the siege trenches.

The army was drawn up in two lines and a reserve, extending a distance of 3,704 paces. There were 11 divisions of foot, consisting of the Garde Française, two Swiss battalions, the regiments of Picardie and Turenne, the Bout de Bois and the four English battalions. The centre of the first line was commanded by the Compte de Gadagne. Seven squadrons were in support to their rear. On the right of the front line were the three divisions of Gassion, D'Esence and Podewiltz, with a detachment of 12 squadrons of horse: the Royal (2), Coislin, Gramont (2), Bouillon, Turenne (2), Coudray, Villette (2) and Podewiltz. The Marquis de Crogney was in command of the squadrons on the right, and Marshal d'Humières those on the left.

The first line of horse was supported on the left by a Bretagne battalion of foot, and on the right by a battalion of Montgomery. Platoons of musketeers from the Bretagne unit were deployed at intervals between the divisions of horse.

To the right of the lines of cavalry 10 squadrons of light horse formed into two brigades, under the Marquis d'Esquancourt and Rochepere, under the overall command of d'Esquancourt.

On the left the Marquis de Castelnau, in overall command, had 13 squadrons under Marquis de Varennes forming his first line, organised into three brigades. The second line under the Compte de Schomberg, consisted of nine squadrons in two brigades under Montclair and Alamont.

---

6   *Ibid.*, p.262.

In reserve were four squadrons of horse under the Marquis de Richelieu, deployed behind the centre of the line. There were ten artillery pieces, six on the right of the foot and four on the left.

Lockhart, on the allied left, was facing the strongly-posted Spanish of Boniface's Regiment, whom he felt 'were posted so advantageously, as, when I considered my work, I looked upon forcing them as altogether impossible.'[7]

Morgan, as we might expect, gives a more dramatic account:

> The next day about eight of the Clock, Marshal Turenne gave Orders to break Avenues on both the Lines, that the Army might March out in Battalia. Major General Morgan set his Soldiers to break Avenues for their marching out in Battalia likewise. Several Officers being with him, as he was looking on his Soldiers at work, Ambassador Lockhart comes up with a white Cap on his head, and said to Major-General Morgan. 'You see what Condition I am in, I am not able to give you any assistance this day. Oh you are the older soldier and the greatest part of the Work of this day must lie upon your Soldiers.' Upon which the Officers smiled and he bid God be with us, and went away with the Lieutenant General of the Horse that was upon our Left Wing. From which time we never saw him till we were in pursuit of the Enemy.
>
> When the Avenues were cleared, both the French and the English Army marched out of the Lines towards the Enemy. We were forced to march in four Lines (for we had not room enough to Wing, for the Canal between Furnes and Dunkirk lay beyond the Sea) till we had marched above half a mile then we came to a Halt on rising Hills of Sand, and having more room took in two of our Lines.
>
> Major-General Morgan seeing the Enemy plain in Battalia, said before the head of the Army 'See yonder are the Gentlemen you have to trade withal.' Upon which the whole Brigade of English gave a shout of rejoicing, that made a roaring Echo betwixt the Sea and the Canal. Thereupon the Marshal Turenne came up with above a hundred Noblemen, to know what was the matter and reason of that Great Shout. Major General Morgan told him, 'T'was a usual Custom of the Redcoats when they saw the Enemy to Rejoice.'
>
> Marshal Turenne answered they were men of Brave Resolution and Courage, after which Marshal Turenne returning to the Head of his Army, we put on to our March again. At the second Halt, the whole Brigade of English gave a Shout and call up their Caps into the Air, saying 'They would have Better Hats before Night'. Marshal Turenne upon that Shout, came up again, with several Noblemen and Officers of the Army, admiring the Resolution of the English, at which time we were within three quarters of a mile of the Enemy in Battalia. Marshal Turenne desired Major General Morgan, that at the next halt, he would keep even front with the French, for, says he 'I do intend to halt at some distance that we may see how the Enemy is drawn up, and take our advantage accordingly.' Major General Morgan demanded of His Excellency whether he would shock the whole Army at one dash, or try one giving fire. Marshal Turenne's reply was 'that as to that Question he could not resolve him yet until he came nearer the Enemy.' Major General Morgan desired the Marshal, not to let him [waiting] for Orders, saying

---

7   Birch, *Thurloe State Papers*, vol. vii, p.128.

THE BATTLE OF THE DUNES

The Battle of the Dunes: a panoramic view.

'that oftentimes Opportunities are lost for want of Orders in due time.' Marshal Turenne said he would either come himself and give Orders or send a Lieutenant General and so Marshal Turenne parted, and went to the Head of his Army. In the meantime Major General Morgan sent orders to the Colonels, and leading Officers, to have a special Care, that when the French came to a halt, they keep even front with them, and further told them, if they could not observe the French, they should take notice when he lifted up his Hat (for he marched little above threescore before the Centre of the Bodies). But when the French came to halt, it so happened, that the English pressed upon their Leading Officers, so that they came up under the shot of the Enemy. But when they saw that Major General Morgan was in a Passion, they put themselves to a stand. Major General Morgan could soon have remedied their Forwardness but he was resolved he would not lose one foot of Ground he had advanced, but would hold it as long as he could.[8]

Some of the English troops were opposite Charles II's Royalists:

[And] we were so near the Enemy, the Soldiers fell into great Friendship, one asking is such an Officer in your Army, another is such a Soldier in yours, and this passed on both sides. Major General Morgan endured this friendship for a little while, then came up to the centre of the Bodies, and demanded how long that friendship would continue, and told them further that for anything they knew, they would be cutting one another's throats within a minute or an hour. The whole Brigade answered 'Their Friends no longer than he pleased.' Then Major General bid them

---

8 Sir Thomas Morgan, *Memoirs*, p.3.

'BETTER BEGGING THAN FIGHTING'

tell the Enemy 'No more Friendship, prepare your Coats and Scarves, for we will be with you sooner than you expect us.'⁹

Just how accurate Morgan was is open to question. Certainly Lockhart gives the clear impression that he was in command, and makes no mention of these incidents. The English foot were between 4,000 and 5,000 strong. Lockhart's, Livingston's, Alsop's and Cochrane's formed the first line, Morgan, Clarke and Pepper the second.

Lieutenant Colonel Richard Hughes bears out Morgan's description of a pause before fighting began:

Typical terrain in the area where the battle took place.

> Our body was come to Thurin (which was 7 miles march) were ordered for the left wing of the army, and horse appointed for our wings. In this posture we marched half a mile where the Spanish army was drawn up in battle array. The Spaniards themselves led by Don John were on the right wing, drawn on a great hill naturally fortified, the Scots and English were next them; Flemish, Walloons and French on the left. Our whole army moving made a stand within half a musket shot of them on another hill without any firing, where they were ordered not to stir until such time as the enemy had quitted the great steep hill.¹⁰

It seems that firing began when a forlorn hope from the Garde Française on the allied right began driving back enemy outposts in the hedges near the canal, but fighting started in earnest on the Allied left when the English troops began an advance. This was sooner than Turenne had intended, as he had planned first to discover as much as he could about the details of the enemy deployment. The English, however were drawn up rather in advance of the rest of the army, within musket shot of the Spanish on the great sand hill. Four hundred firelocks who had been deployed among the French horse on the beach were recalled and ordered to fire on the two inaccessible sides of the sand hill, while the main force made a frontal assault.

James Duke of York described the opening moves as viewed from the Spanish side:

> The first who engaged us were the English led up by Major General Morgan their General Lockhart (for what reason I know not) being with Major General de Castelnau at the head of their left wing. But immediately before their falling on, Don John sent, and desired me to go to our right hand, and take a particular

---

9 *Ibid.*
10 Firth, *The Clarke Papers*, vol. III, p.151.

care of that part, where he saw the English were advancing. Which I did, taking no troops along with me from the middle of the Line, where I was, excepting my own Troop of Guards. And a hundred commanded men, with two captains, and Officers proportionable out of my next battalion, to reinforce the natural Spaniards. Which Foot (from the King's Regiment of Foot) I joined to Boniface, where I judged they would make their greatest effort, and which was the greatest importance to be maintained, it being the highest of the sand hills on that side, and advanced somewhat further than the rest of than any of the rest of them which were thereabout, commanding also those which were nearest to it.[11]

Lockhart said: 'necessity having no law, I ordered my own regiment to attempt it before, and at the same time, having some commanded foot upon the strand, which were to have seconded the horse I made them attack the Spanish upon the flank.'[12]

Another account gives more details of this forlorn hope 'consisting of half of his excellency the Lord Ambassador's regiment, and part of that commanded by lieutenant colonel Haines, was led on by Lieutenant-Colonel Fennerick [Fenwick], his excellency's lieutenant-colonel.'[13]

Lieutenant Colonel Hughes explained that 'Our men could not be kept in without engaging, went into the valley without orders being given (yea, contrary to orders) and on hands and knees crept up the hill.'[14]

As might be expected, Morgan's version of events is the fullest and most dramatic. The enemy opened fire first, and:

> Poured a volley of Shot into one of our Battalions wounded three or four, and one dropped. The Major General immediately sent the Adjutant General to Marshal Turenne for Orders, whether he should charge the Enemy's right wing, or whether Marshal Turenne would engage the Enemies' left wing and advised the Adjutant-General not to stay, but to acquaint Marshal Turenne, that we were under the enemies' shot, and had received some prejudice already. But there was no return of the Adjutant General nor Orders.
>
> By and by the Enemy poured in another volley of shot, into another of our battalions, and wounded two or three. Major General Morgan observing the Enemy mending Faults, and opening the intervals of the Foot, to bring Horse in, which would have made our work more difficult, called all the Colonels and Officers of the Field together, before the Centre of the Bodies, and told them he had sent the Adjutant-General for Orders. But when he saw there was no hope of orders, he told them if they would concur with him, he would immediately charge the Enemies' right Wing. Their answer was: 'They were ready whenever he gave orders.'
>
> He told them, he would try the right wing with the Blue Regiment and the four hundred Firelocks which were in the intervals of the French horse, and warned all the Field Officers to be ready at their several posts.

---

11 Sells, *Memoirs of James II*, p.263.
12 Birch, *Thurloe State Papers*, op. cit.
13 *Mercurius Politicus*, no. 421, 17–24 June 1658, p.619.
14 Firth, *The Clarke Papers*, op. cit.

'BETTER BEGGING THAN FIGHTING'

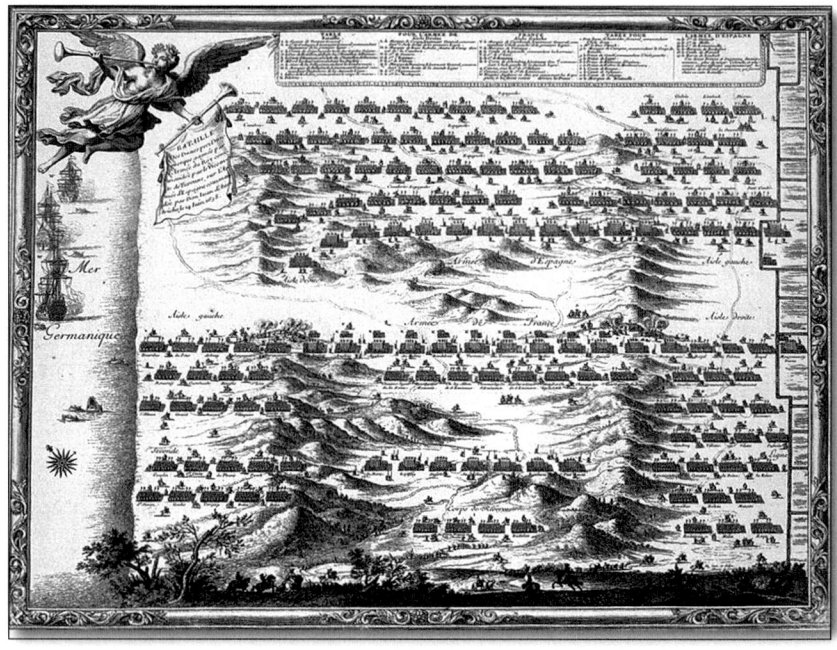

A contemporary plan of the battle.

Major General Morgan gave orders that the other Five Regiments should not move from their Ground, except they saw the Blue regiment, the White, and the four hundred firelocks, shocked the enemies' right wing off of their Ground, and further showed the several Colonels what Colours they were to charge, and told them moreover that if he was not knocked on the head, he would come to them. In like manner as fast as he could, he admonished the whole Brigade, and told them, they were to look in the face of an Enemy who had violated and endeavoured to take away their reputation, and that they had no way but to fight it out to the last man or to be killed, taken prisoner or drowned, and further, that the Honour of England did depend much upon their Gallantry and resolution that Day.

The Enemies' Wing was posted on a Sandy Hill. And had cast up a work breast high before them. Then General Morgan did order the Blue Regiment and the four hundred firelocks to advance to the Charge. In the meantime Major General Morgan knowing the Enemy would all bend upon them that did advance, removed the White Regiment more to the right, that it might be in the Flank of them, by that time the Blue Regiment was got within push of pike.[15]

The Duke of York said that:

The English came on with great eagerness and courage. But their heat was such, that they outmarched the French, so that had the opportunity been taken, they might have paid dear for their rash bravery. But they, whose business it was to have take that advantage, either took no notice of it, or had some other reason, unknown to me, why they sent not some Horse to fall into their Flanks.

---

15   Sir Thomas Morgan, *Memoirs*, pp.4–5.

THE BATTLE OF THE DUNES

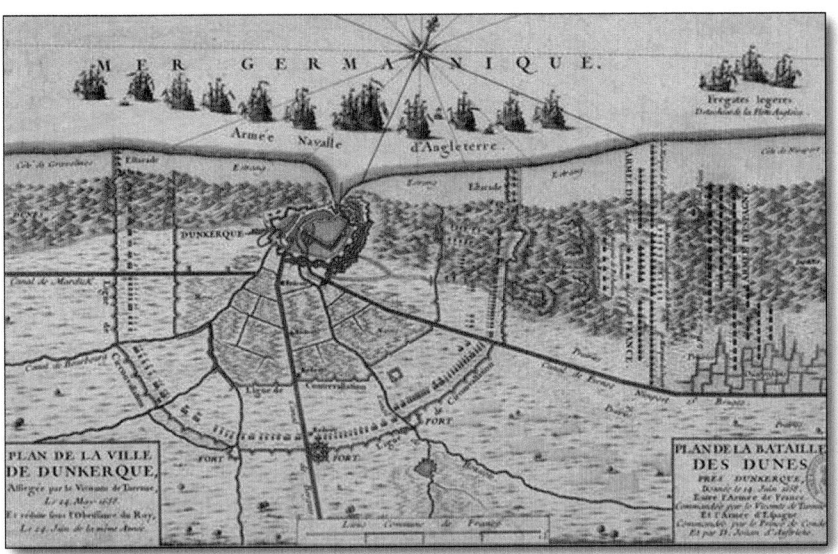

Another contemporary plan.

Whatsoever the occasion was, the opportunity was let slip, and the English came up without the least disturbance to make their charge.

Boniface, as I have already said, was posted on the highest Sand hill, which was somewhat advanced before any of the others, so that the battle began there. It was Lockhart's own Regiment which charged those Spaniards, and was commanded by Lieutenant Colonel Fenwick. Who so soon as he came to the bottom of the hill, seeing that it was exceedingly steep, and difficult to ascend, commanded his men to halt and take breath for two or three minutes, that they might be more able to climb and do their duty.

While they were thus preparing themselves, their commanded men opening to the right and left, to give way for their main body which was to mount the height, were continually firing at Boniface, and as soon as the body were in a condition to climb, they began their ascent with a great shout, which was general from all their foot. But while they were scrambling up in the best manner they were able, the Lieutenant Colonel fell in the middle way, being shot through the body; which yet hindered not the Major, who was called Hinton (since a Captain in the Duke of Albemarle's Regiment) from leading on his men together with the rest of the Officers, who stopped not till they came to push of pike. Where, notwithstanding the great resistance which was made by the Spaniards, and the advantage they had of higher ground, as well as, that of being well in breath, when their Enemies were almost spent with climbing, the English gained the hill and drove them from off it. The Spaniards leaving dead upon the spot, seven of eleven captains who commanded in the Regiment, together with Slaughter and Farrell, two Captains whom I had joined to that Regiment just before. Besides many of their reformed [reformado] officers (their stands of Pikes being for the most part made of such). Yet this ground had been so well disputed, that the English, besides their Lieutenant Colonel, lost several officers and soldiers.[16]

---

16 Sells, *Memoirs of James II*, pp.263–4.

Lieutenant Colonel Hughes said that the hill was so steep that the men had to climb it on their hands and knees, and on reaching the top, delivered a volley, then engaged the enemy with musket butt and pike.

Another account details the English losses, among them:

> A noble young gentleman, Mr Henry Jones of Oxfordshire, a volunteer ... Who was shot through the body. Fenwick was shot through the body, and Jones shot through the shoulder, and wounded in two other places ... Colonel Daniel had one horse shot under him, and being with difficulty remounted, was pushed off by a pike, but is not wounded. The English acted miracles in this battle.[17]

James Duke of York saw that the situation was critical. The whole right flank of the Spanish army was under threat. As the English reformed, and came down the sand hill in pursuit of Boniface's men:

> I ... went to charge them with my own Guards and those of Don Juan, but being come up almost within reach of their pikes, I found the ground to be such, as rendered it almost impossible for me to break into them. Notwithstanding which I was ready I was resolved to endeavour it, and accordingly charged them though to no purpose, for what with the advantage of the ground, and with the stout resistance they made in that first charge, I was beaten off, and all who were at the head of my own Troop, were either killed or wounded, of which number I had been one, had not the goodness of my arms preserved me. The chief Officers of my Troop escaped better than those belonging to Don Juan, for of mine, only Charles Berkeley, the Captain of my Guards was hurt, and of the other, only the Count de Colmenar who was Captain of it, came off unwounded, amongst all the officers. Neither did their common men fare better, the loss falling so heavily amongst them that though I endeavoured all I could to rally them, it was not possible for me to perform it. but I had better fortune with those of my own Guards, for I got all of them together who were yet in a condition of doing duty, which were not above forty.
>
> When I had rallied this small party, I went to Boniface, where first Don Juan, and after him the Marquis de Caracena, had been endeavouring to rally them, but not being able to do it, were gone off. When I came up to that Regiment, I was not able at first to make them stand, but while I was trying my authority amongst them, I saw there one Elvige a Lieutenant of the King's regiment, who had been commanded along with the hundred men whom I had sent to strengthen that Battalion. And asking him, what was become of his Captains? He answered me, they were both slain with most of their Soldiers, and that he was the only Officer of that party that had escaped unhurt. Upon which I commanded him to stay with me, and call his men together, which he did, and crying out aloud to them. That the Duke was there, those who heard him faced about immediately, and came up to us. At the same time, seeing the Major of the Spanish Regiment, I called to him that he should make his men follow the example of those few English, it not being the custom of Spaniards to run away when any others stood. And

---

17 *Mercurius Politicus*, op. cit.

upon the Major's reproaching them with that, they stopped, and drew up in good order. And now the Marquis of Caracena, coming back once more, demanded of me, Why I charged not the Enemy with my Horse? I answered him, I had already done it and [been] worsted for my pains; further telling him, that considering the present posture of the Enemy, it was impossible to be done, and at the same time showing him, what I had affirmed, from behind the next Sand hill.

Presently after this (the Marquis being gone again) Lockhart's Regiment, which, as I have already said, had beaten off our Horse, advanced not directly forward, but bent a little towards their left hand; and we lost sight of each other, by reason of the unevenness of the ground (a Sand hill being interposed betwixt us) so that by the time I had got the Regiment of Boniface in order, and those few Horse which I had with him, this English battalion was come even upon a line with us, just upon my right hand, a Sand hill only being betwixt us. Whereupon I faced towards the Sea, and marching at the head of my Foot, as I came up to the top of the Sand hill, I perceived the head of the English coming up on the other side to me. Upon which I got from betwixt them, commanding the major who was with me at the head of Boniface. To charge them in the front, whilst I with my Horse would fall into their flank.

When I had given this order, I put myself immediately at the head of my forty Guards, and charged that Battalion so home, that I broke into them, doing great execution upon them, and driving them to the edge of the Sand hill next the Strand. As for the Battalion of Boniface, they did not charge, seeing I had already broken the English; but discovering from the top of the sand hill, where they were, that our whole army was in rout, they scattered, and every man endeavoured to get off, which few of them were so lucky as to perform.

Tis very observable that when we had broken into this Battalion, and were got amongst them, not so much as one single man of them ask'd quarter, or threw down his arms. But every one of them defended himself to the last, so that we ran as great danger by the butt end of their muskets, as by the volley which they had given us. And one of them had infallibly knocked me off from my horse, if I had not prevented him when he was just ready to have discharged his blow, by a stroke I gave him with my sword over the face, which laid him along upon the ground.

The Duke of Gloucester, who during the action of all that day had seconded me, and behaved himself as bravely as any of his Ancestors had ever done, had his sword either struck out of his hand by one of the enemy, or it flew out of his hand by a blow which he had given, but which of the two I remember not. It happened that a gentleman, one Villeneuve, Ecuier to the Prince de Ligny, who was next to him, saw this accident, whereupon he leapt down from his horse, took up the sword and delivered it to my Brother, who with his pistol in his hand, stood ready to secure him until he remounted. But immediately after, the same gentleman was shot through the body. Notwithstanding which it was his fortune to get off, and to recover of his wound.[18]

---

18 Sells, *Memoirs of James II*, pp.265–7.

The English version of this counterattack, perhaps understandably, is briefer. Lieutenant Colonel Hughes wrote that after giving Boniface's Regiment 'two good volleys' and forcing them back with their pikes:

> Don Juan with his horse gave the General's Regiment and Colonel Lillingston's a violent charge, that they were forced to give ground a little confusedly, but soon rallied, and forced Don Juan to retreat with the loss of his foot and many of his horse. The French horse appointed for our wings standing still without giving the least assistance till they saw the enemy routed, having no stomach to fight.[19]

French accounts however, suggest that a flank attack by the horse under Castelnau on the Spanish cavalry at the rear of the sand hill was the decisive act. Certainly the French cavalry advancing along the beach did see off the Spanish horse, though the English accounts place this action after the battle for the sand hill had been won. That in *Mercurius Politicus* says:

> Then the enemie's horse charged that party of our men with some prejudice to them, but we following them close and coming up to the reserve, the Count de Schomberg came and told us that he would Bond us with a reserve of horse, which he did accordingly, and they came up to second us. And here the enemy was so warmly plied by our united forces that they immediately betook themselves to their heels.

Another account, however, says that Schomberg's support came after the sandhill had been taken until when 'there was not a Frenchman that engaged.'[20]

Colonel Drummond said of this stage of the battle 'Fenwick, the General's Lieutenant Colonel, is wounded very dangerously, two captains killed, one Captain Johns that commanded the horse at Jamaica wounded and taken prisoner by the enemy by engaging too far. Next Colonel Lillingston's had the hardest pull, where there are thirty or forty killed.'[21]

Morgan wrote that James Duke of York's counterattack:

> Exposed his Person to great danger. But we knew nobody at that time. Immediately the enemy were clear shocked off their ground, and the English Colours flying over their Heads, the strongest Officers and Soldiers clubbing them down. Major General Morgan, when he saw his opportunity, leapt to the other five Regiments which were within six score [yards] of him, and ordered them to advance, and charge immediately.[22]

The Anglo-French forces were now attacking all along, with alarm at the collapse of their right wing rapidly spreading down the Spanish line. The Duke of York witnessed what was happening:

---

19 Firth, *The Clarke Papers, op. cit.*
20 *Mercurius Politicus, op. cit.*
21 Birch, *Thurloe State Papers*, vol. vii, p.127.
22 Sir Thomas Morgan, *Memoirs*, p.7.

I had no sooner made this charge, but I was obliged to make what haste I could to get away; for a Squadron of the French Army from the Strand, had got up amongst the Sand hills, just as I was charging, and had attacked my flank. So that they had undoubtedly cut me off with my small party, had they not been charged themselves, at the same time, by the Prince de Ligne, who though he did not defeat them, yet he gave them a little stop; which opportunity I took to get off, and the Prince, after he had made his charge, escaped another way.

By this time not only the Regiment of Boniface was cut in pieces, but the rest of the natural Spanish Regiments were all taken in their several posts by the Horse, for they were not charged by the English as they ought to have been, had our Countrymen marched directly onwards. But it so happened, that when the other two Regiments of them, saw the resistance which was made by Boniface, they all bent that way, marching by the flank, only firing at the other natural Spaniards as they passed along, and marching up the Sand hill after Lockhart's Regiment.'[23]

French accounts make much more of the part which they claim their forces played, along with the English, in the defeat of the Spanish right. While the English foot were engaged in hand to hand combat with Boniface's, Castelnau ordered French guns brought up to within pistol shot of the Spanish and opened fire on the right flank of the Spanish foot and the cavalry to their rear, while two squadrons under the Compte de Longville made a frontal attack.

The Duke of York's counterattack was countercharged on its left flank by Castelnau and his horse, consisting of three regiments of horse and the brigade under the Marquis de Varennes. With York in retreat, the Lorraine cavalry then charged the flank of the Spanish foot under attack from the English, and broke them, taking 2,000 prisoners. Joined by fresh troops from the first and second lines, they completed the rout of the Spanish right, chasing them to within sight of Nieuport. Some of the Spaniards, attempting to flee along the open beach, were cut to pieces by the French horse.

The attack on the centre and left of the Spanish army began at about the same time. In the centre, covered by forlorn hopes of musketeers, the regiments of Bout de Bras, Turenne, Picardie and the Garde Française advanced. One volley proved enough to put Caracena's men to flight, without making serious resistance. Only Condé's guards imposed a brief check on a detachment of Garde Française, but the Compte de Soissons, sword in hand, at the head of a battalion of Swiss guards broke Condé's men in a fierce charge.

However, Condé again managed to check the French advance. He now had the Garde Française, the Swiss and the Musketeers du Roi on his right flank, advancing into the gap left by the rout of Caracena's men in the centre. He had been preparing to attack the French horse in the meadows on the Allied right, which were in a holding position. But now the rather rash advance of the Garde Française had left their right flank open and Condé

---

23 Sells, *Memoirs of James II*, p.267.

charged them. His horse came under heavy fire, and Condé himself twice narrowly escaped capture.

The Duke of York described the collapse of the Spanish centre and left:

> While these things were passing on our right hand next the Sea, our left wing received as hard measure from the enemy as we had done; for the four field pieces, which, as I said, advanced along the highway, under the Sand hills, terribly galled both our horse and Foot which were before them. So that the Foot Guards [Garde Française] and the Regiment de la Couronne (the last of which was commanded by Monsieur de Montgomery, and having been taken out of the Second Line by Monsieur de Turenne, as I have said, was placed on the right hand of the Guards in the meadow grounds) seeing that we had three small Battalions betwixt the Sand hills and the Canal, they advanced against them, but our Battalions making a very faint resistance ran away. Upon which the French horse advanced before their foot, as many Squadrons a front as they could march, commanded by the Marquis de Crequi, a Lieutenant General, and were charged so vigorously by the Prince of Conde's horse, that they were beaten back behind their foot. Yet at length, notwithstanding all he could do, they having horse and foot against horse alone, they forced him from his ground, and obliged him to run for it, as fast as his neighbours had done before him, though he did what was possible to be done, in both capacities, both as a General and a Soldier, in so much that at the last of the three charges, he was in great hazard of being taken.
>
> As to what passed on the right wing of the Prince of Conde [the Spanish centre] upon the Sand hills betwixt him and the place where the natural Spaniards were drawn up. The Regiment de Guiault (which was posted upon the Sand hill next to the highway along which came the right wing of the French cavalry) did not stay for a charge from the Swiss, but fired at too great a distance and presently ran away. The Four next Battalions did the like, none of them staying to be thoroughly charged, which cowardice of theirs, and the defeat of Boniface his Regiment, who were beaten from their ground, struck such a terror into our horse, which were drawn up behind our foot on the Sand hills, that the greatest part of them, especially those of the second line, ran away without being charged, or even without seeing an Enemy, though most of their Officers were not wanting in their duty, in endeavouring to stop them. Those few who had courage enough to stay, performed their parts like men of honour, as shall be mentioned in its proper place.
>
> The next of these three Regiments, of which I have spoken, was my own, which stood a little longer than their neighbours on the left hand. But a voice coming behind them, that the foot should save themselves, that Battalion broke also, the Soldiers leaving their Officers, and running away. Which Colonel Grace seeing, who was drawn up behind them, thought it was high time for him to endeavour to save his Regiment, and march off in good order at a round rate in three divisions, by observing of which disciple, and keeping them together, he had the good fortune to get off across the highway, to the Canal of Furnes, along which he made his retreat without losing a man. But my Regiment was attended with worse luck, for though Monsieur de St Roch with his Regiment of Horse went up and charged the Cardinal's Gendarmes, killing with his own hand Monsieur de Bourg who commanded them, and beating that Squadron, yet they

who should have seconded him being gone, and more horse coming on to charge him, he was forced also to make the best of his way, and shift for one. Those horse which he had beaten soon overtook my Regiment, so that excepting My Lord Muskerry, who was fortunate enough to get a horse accidentally, not a Soldier or Officer escaped.

Much about the same time, one Michel an old German Colonel, with his Regiment of Horse, charged the Battalion of Turenne after they were marched down from the hill, on which the Spanish foot had been drawn up, but he was not able to break them, they receiving his charge in so good order, that they killed him with the greatest part of his Officers, and beat off his regiment of horse without any loss but of Lieutenant Colonel Bebese, who was slain at the head of the pikes with a pistol shot. Besides these two Colonels, I know not of any Spanish horse that behaved themselves well in this battle. Or if they did, it never arrived to my knowledge.[24]

Lieutenant Colonel Hughes told General Monck that he was not impressed with the performance of most of Charles II's army:

The Duke of York's English, Middleton's Scotch and Ormond's Irish were soon beaten, the English only fighting. The Scots and Irish, as our regiment and Colonel Alsop's were coming up to them, veiled their colours, and made show of yielding, but ours judging it a defiance as they had done before we moved, gave fire at them, but it was very real, for they had laid down their arms, and cried for quarter, and on our firing they struggled a little, and were soon quelled, all being killed and taken. Amongst whom it is reported my Lord Musgrave was slain and several English Gentlemen. Such as we met of our runaways [deserters from the English expedition] were knock't on the head, and such as we met amongst the French were forced from them, and intend to do justice on them.[25]

The Duke of York described the much sterner fight put up by King Charles' Regiment of Foot:

I have not yet given an account of the Battalion, which was composed of the King's Regiment and The Earl of Bristol's, and I should be very injurious to the finest of these two, if I should pass them by in silence. They were posted, as I have said, next the natural Spaniards; and notwithstanding that they saw all on the right and left hand of them already routed and gone off, yet they continued firm (I mean that part of the Battalion which was composed of the King's Regiment) for they were all English. As for the other part of it, which was formed of My Lord of Bristol's men who were Irish, they indeed went away, when they saw all their friends about them beaten. Neither was it in the power of their Officers to hinder them, though they endeavoured it, but seeing their pains were to no effect, they ran for company, excepting Captain Stroud an English Gentleman, who was

---

24 *Ibid.*, pp.267–9.
25 Firth, *The Clarke Papers, op. cit.*

Captain Lieutenant of that Regiment; for he came and put himself at the head of the remaining part of the battalion with his own countrymen.

But this was not the only discouragement which these English had, for both the Lieutenant Colonel and the Major had forsaken them before the Irish, the first upon pretence of going for orders, and the other upon an account which was not a jot more honourable. The Lieutenant Colonel was rewarded for his pains as he deserved, for being met by some of the loose French horse, who were then got behind them, he was shot in the face, somewhat below the eye, and the bullet came out behind his neck, of which wound he narrowly escaped with life. He was also unhorsed, and being in this condition, one of my Guards, the only man amongst them who behaved himself ill, and who was not an Englishman, accidentally found him, and helped him off.

But none of these misadventures did at all daunt the King's Regiment. They continued to stand firm, and maintained their ground, though they beheld the first Line of the French passing by them on their left hand, and the Cromwellian English on the right, till the second Line came up to them. It was the Regiment of Rambures which advanced to charge them (their Colonel commanding that line and being at their head). This Officer seeing not a man standing of all our Troops, excepting this small body which was before him, went up to them himself, a little before his men, to offer them quarter. To whom they returned this answer, That they had been posted there by the Duke, and therefore were resolved to maintain that ground as long as they were able. He replied that it would be to no purpose for them to stand out, their whole Army being already routed, and having left the field. They answered again, That it was not their part to believe an Enemy. Upon which he offered them, that if they would send out an Officer or two, he would himself carry them up to a Sand hill which was behind them, and then they should perceive, that what he affirmed was true. Accordingly they sent out two Officers, Captain Thomas Cooke and Aston, whom he conducted as he had promised to the Sand hill which he had named; from whence they could easily discover, that none of our Army was left standing excepting only themselves, after which, he brought them down again to their own men. Whereupon they told him, That in case he would promised that they would not be delivered up to the English, nor be stripped, nor have their pockets searched, they would lay down their arms and yield themselves his prisoners; to which he immediately agreeing, and giving his word for the performance of those Articles, they accordingly yielded, and his promise was exactly kept to them. By which their honourable carriage, they fared much better than the other Regiment which deserted them; some of whom were slain, and the rest taken and stripped afterwards.[26]

Lieutenant John Gwynne, who was present, also described the incident, saying that the French commander offered honourable conditions 'with high applause for our resolution to stand the field when all had left us.' Amongst those captured were Colonel Carles, Major Beversham, Ensign Crispe, and Mr Rudston 'our surgeon.' These, with Gwynne went with the captain who had offered terms, unlike, Gwynne claims the rest of the regiment, which

---

26 Sells, *Memoirs of James II*, pp.271–3.

THE BATTLE OF THE DUNES

Turenne at the Battle of the Dunes.

would have been better to have followed their example, rather than 'go away in parcels, as they did, to the great sorrow of some and death of several.'[27]

James Duke of York had to make his own escape:

> As soon as I came off from charging and breaking that Regiment of English, I thought it but reasonable to endeavour my own escape, the French horse having already encompassed me on every side, and none of our men standing. But not knowing what success we might have had in our left wing where the Prince of Conde was, I resolved in the first place to go thither, and see in what posture our affairs were there. I had not now above twenty horse remaining with me, the rest of my Guards which were with my Lieutenant, being parted from me as I came from amongst the English. The smallness of my number proved my best security, for with those who still continued about me, I was strong enough to deal with any loose men, and yet was not so considerable as to provoke any bodies to disband after me. And by some of the Enemy we were taken for one of their own parties, for as I was coming off, I saw four or five of their Troopers falling upon an Officer of mine, one Lieutenant Victor, since a Captain at Tangier. I went up to them, taking them indeed for some of our own horse, and called out to them in French, that they should let him alone, for he was one of our own Englishmen. Accordingly they dismissed him, giving him his sword which they had taken from him, and went off themselves, mistaking me for one of their own Officers. Thus both I and they were in an error, and I knew not my own mistake till Victor told me of it afterwards.

---

27 Sir Thomas Morgan, *Memoirs*, pp.7–8.

I continued my way forward, and made a shift to pass through the French, trotting in good order, till I overtook Colonel Grace and his Regiment before they got out from amongst the Sand hills, going by the Regiments of Picardy and Turenne, which were then as far advanced as where our men had been encamped the night before; and coming down into the high way, under the sand hills, I found all of the Prince of Conde's Troops already beaten, he having then made his last charge. So that he was constrained to run with them, and as I said, with great difficulty escaped. The throng being very great in the village of Zudcote, through which the high way went, and the enemy pursuing us with great eagerness, I had no other means to avoid being taken, than to disengage myself from the crowd, and to take another way, which was round about the village leaving it on my right hand. And to show how near I was to be made prisoner, a Colonel under the Prince, one de Morieul, meeting me just as I came down the Sand hills, and not following my example of taking round the Village, but mingling with the crowd, immediately after he was parted from me fell into the hands of the pursuers, and was made a prisoner. As for me, I got safe into the way again on the other side of the Village, where Don Juan, the Prince of Conde, the Marquis de Caracena, and others, were already got before me. Soon after which, we were obliged to make a little stand, and face about, to give Don Juan the leisure to change his horse, his own by some accident being fallen lame. Which being done, we set spurs again to our horses, and did not stop, till the Enemy had left pursuing us.[28]

Thomas Morgan gave a colourful, if extremely biased, account of the closing stages of the battle; when the English foot advanced towards the remaining Spaniards, after the defeat of Boniface's regiment:

When they came within ten pikes length, the Enemy perceiving they were not able to endure our Charge, some their Hats held up, the Spanish their handkerchiefs, and called for Quarter, but the Redcoats cried aloud, they had no care for Quarter, Whereupon the Enemy faced about, and would not endure or Charge, but fell to run, having the English Colours over their heads, and the strongest Soldiers and Officers clubbing them down, so that the six thousand English carried ten or Twelve Thousand Horse and Foot before them. The French Army was about Musket-shot in the rear of us, and came on with much Gallantry, but they never struck one stroke, only carried Prisoners back to Camp. Neither did we see Ambassador Mr Lockhart, till we were in pursuit of the enemy, and then we could see him amongst us very brisk, without his white Cap on his Head, and neither troubled with Gravel or Stones.[29]

Morgan was clearly motivated by dislike of Lockhart, and his insinuations of cowardice are not supported by other reports, which said that French officers were full of praise for Lockhart: 'They infinitely esteem my lord Lockhart for his courage, care and enduring the fatigue beyond all the men they ever saw.'[30] Morgan's dismissal of French contributions to the victory is

---

28 Sells, *Memoirs of James II*, pp.269–70.
29 Sir Thomas Morgan, *Memoirs*, pp.9–10.
30 *Mercurius Politicus, op. cit.*

equally ill-founded. There was however apparently a widely held view among the English soldiers that without them the French would have been beaten, and a feeling that the French horse on the left had done little to support them. Lieutenant Colonel Hughes felt that:

> All their foot being near 5,000 are killed or taken. York's horse was killed and Charles is left without 20 men to invade England of his own. Had Turenne's horse done any service at all, the whole army would have been killed and taken, having three mile of good ground to pursue them, the enemy being in a great confusion, but the French horse would pursue not one step further than our foot went. And thus through God's great goodness we have been instrumental and the real actors of gaining this seasonable victory, which we trust we shall make good use of. Had we not engaged, the French would have been soundly banged, and the town relieved, which the Spaniards were confident of.[31]

Colonel Drummond claimed that the English foot:

> Charged first, and so fell in betwixt our right wing (or rather the enemies' left wing) and the town of Furnes that was their retreat, so that if the horse of our wing had pursued so vigorously as we expected, the enemys' left wing and the Prince [Condé] had been ours; but so it was that most part of all their horse did escape, but the foot, who was but some five thousand, are all gone, whereof we have about two thousand prisoners, but of officers of horse and foot we have eight hundred.[32]

The French only pursued the retreating enemy as far as the pontoon bridges over the Canal, while their main force, and the English concentrated on rounding up enemy stragglers in the sand hills and a large number who were unable to cross the Canal.

Allied casualties amounted to 300–400 men, most of them English. According to Lieutenant Colonel Hughes, whose figures include some casualties suffered in the siegeworks: 'we lost at the battle four captains, four lieutenants, and not 50 men, one colonel, one major, wounded, with most of the officers. We have two captains, six lieutenants, twelve sergeants of our regiment wounded desperately in the battle and approaches. Little Captain Sherwin with his lieutenant and ensign were slain in the field.'[33]

Lockhart said that in his own regiment only one captain, a captain lieutenant, and some ensigns, lieutenants and a sergeant were not killed or dangerously wounded. He ended his report, written immediately after the battle: 'The truth is, my lord, I have fallen asleep, I know not how often, in writing this.'[34]

Morgan, one feels, would have had a caustic comment.

The Duke of York attempted a more detailed breakdown of casualties:

---

31 Firth, *The Clarke Papers*, op. cit.
32 Birch, *Thurloe State Papers*, vol. vii, pp.126, 156, 160; Green, *CSPD Commonwealth 1658–9*, p.97.
33 Firth, *The Clarke Papers*, vol. III, p.154.
34 Birch, *Thurloe State Papers*, vol. vii, p.127.

I have now given the best account I am able of the whole Action, and it remains, that I should say something of the number of slain on both sides and of the prisoners. As for the slain, they amounted in all to not above four hundred [probably just referring to the Spanish and Royalist forces] amongst which on our side there fell the Count de la Motterie and of the Spanish troops, Colonel Michel, with most of the Captains of Boniface, one of Seravlo, and another of Gomez, as also Don Francisco Romero Governor of the two Troops of Guards, with two or three more of his Officers. Of those whom I commanded, there were killed three Captains, Slaughter of the King's Regiment, ----- of my own, and Farrell of the Lord Bristol's, besides some Lieutenants and Ensigns, and two Brigadiers of my Troop of Guards. Of the Prince of Conde's Troops, I remember none of quality but the Count de Meille, a Lieutenant General, with some few Captains. Of the Spanish Officers, were taken the Marquis de Seralvo, Risbourg, Conflans, Belleveder, the Prince de Tobec, Don Antonio de Cordova, Don Juan de Toledo of Portugal, Don Joseph Manriques, Don Luis de Zuniga, Le Baron de Limbeck, Darchem, Batnes, all Colonels of horse or foot, And Mr de Montmorency, Captain of the Guards to the Prince de Ligne.

Most of these were abandoned by their men, and were taken, because they would not make such haste away as their Soldiers had done. I cannot say what Captains and other inferior Officers were made Prisoners, only, that of the natural Spanish Regiments of foot, few or none escaped, because they behaved themselves very honourably. But of the horse, the numbers of Captains and Officers under them, was no way proportionable to the number of Officers in my Troops. Of my own Regiment, not an officer escaped taking, excepting my Lord Muskerry, who commanded it; and of the private soldiers, not twenty. As for the King's Regiment, it was entirely broken. The Earl of Bristol's Regiment had the same fate with mine, few or none getting away; but of his Guards not above five or six were taken.

As for the Chief Officers under the Prince of Conde, Monsieur de Coligny and Boutteville, both Lieutenant Generals, were made Prisoners with Meille (who died of his wounds) and Mons. Des Roches, Captain of his Guards. He lost not many of his foot, for they not doing their duty as became Soldiers, and being near the Canal, had an easy opportunity of escaping. His horse, though they fought bravely, yet lost fewer than the Spaniards, and amongst them all not one Colonel.

How many of the Enemy were slain, the Duke knew not certainly, only in general, that their loss was very inconsiderable both as to the number and the quality, for I have not heard of any other Officers who were killed on their side, than Monsr. De la Berge (who had been Captain of Mr de Turenne's Guards, and was then Major General of the Foot …) Monsr. de Brebsey, Lieutenant Colonel of Mons de Turenne's Regiment of Foot, and Du Bourg, Lieutenant of the Cardinal's Gendarmes. Of the English sent by Cromwell, Fenwick, Lockhart's Lieutenant Colonel, with two Captains, four Lieutenants, and four Ensigns. Of the English common men, about a hundred, and the Major of the same Regiment, with two Captains and some Lieutenants and Ensigns hurt.

> As for the baggage and cannon, we had none to lose our train by good fortune not being come up to us; and our baggage being left behind at Furnes, at which place we rallied our beaten army.[35]

If James himself had fallen into English hands, his fate would have been extremely uncertain. He explains:

> And here I must not forget to mention, what Monsr. De Gadagne, a Lieutenant general in the French Army, and who commanded the French Foot that day, did on my behalf, when our army was entirely routed, and none left standing on the field, hearing that I was taken prisoner by the English, he took two or three Squadrons of the French horse along with him, whose Commanders were his particular Friends, and went with them across the field to the place where the English then were; fully resolved, in case my fortune had been such, to have rescued me by force out of their hands. But coming amongst them, and after a diligent inquiry finding there was no truth in that report, he returned back with that satisfaction to his own command.[36]

It seems likely that allied estimates of a total Spanish casualty list of about 5,000, the majority of them prisoners, was roughly accurate. Colonel Drummond told General Monck 'the foot, who was but some five thousand, are all gone, whereof we have about two thousand prisoner, but of officers of horse and foot we have eight hundred.'[37] The majority of the 'natural' Spanish foot had been captured. It was, of course, usual practice to exchange prisoners if sufficient were available. But Turenne, knowing of Don Juan's critical shortage of foot, and the virtual impossibility of his replacing any of his natural Spanish, generally regarded as the cream of his foot, refused to exchange any of them:

> All those that are of the old Spanish regiments of Flanders the King of France has taken them to put in prison in France; they would willingly give their ransom, but the King has ordered his Commissaries that are here to pay their ransoms to those that took them and that he will not part with them, and the reason is that the King of Spain hath not any Spanish now in Flanders that know the way of war in Flanders now, or that have any reputation of the country for making new levies, and that he will hardly be induced to trust the nobility of the country with military commands.[38]

Many of the Walloon prisoners were sent to serve German princes. The fate of the rank and file of Charles II's men who were captured is not specifically recorded, but it is likely that they were recruited into the French army, where many of them had served previously.

---

35 Sells, *Memoirs of James II*, pp.274–5.
36 *Ibid.*, p.274.
37 Firth, *The Clarke Papers, op. cit.*
38 Birch, *Thurloe State Papers*, vol. vii, p.160.

The officers of King Charles' army were on the whole treated more generously. Lieutenant John Gwynne of the King's Regiment of Foot, who had been captured with some of his fellow officers, remembered that the French captain in whose charge they were placed, fed them 'with the provisions he had at present', supplied them with money for their immediate needs, and contracting for a half of their ransom, let them go on parole and 'like a brave Breton as he was, to crown the rest of his civilities produced a whole cluster of bottles of wine from under some [of their escorts'] cloaks, which we sacrificed in the remembrance of princes, till we were almost all so unconcerned, and fortified us purely to neglect those great water plashes we waded through and the broad deep ditches we mounted over, sometimes near drowning with want of top staves,' until eventually they safely rejoined the Duke of York at Nieuport.[39]

Turenne pithily summarised his victory in a letter that evening to his wife: 'The enemy came to us and God be praised they have been defeated. I was pretty busy all day, which has fatigued me. I wish you goodnight. I am going to bed.'

---

39 Tucker and Young, Gwynne's *Military Memoirs, op. cit.*

8

The Fall of Dunkirk

Even while the prisoners were being rounded up after the battle, Turenne ordered back some of the French troops to help hold the siegeworks before Dunkirk. However they were in disorder, and 'celebrating', probably by plundering the dead and prisoners, so it took time for the Duc de Richelieu to muster as many as he could. As he approached the siege lines, Richelieu saw fires burning in his and the English camp. The Dunkirk garrison had taken the opportunity to make a sortie, and five squadrons of horse were drawn up covering the foot who were burning Lockhart's tent and killing some of the English wounded in the camp. Richelieu chased the Spaniards back within their defences, taking a number of prisoners.

Despite the failure of the relief attempt, the Governor of Dunkirk remained defiant, saying that he would rather die than see the town in the hands of the English, and would fight to the last man. The garrison demonstrated their defiance on the night of 15/16 June by making a sortie, which was met with heavy fire by the besiegers, illuminating the attackers by the light of burning torches. On the following night (17/18 June) it was the turn of the besiegers to take the offensive, attacking at five points. Two battalions of Turenne's Regiment gained some ground at the cost of 200 men, whilst on the same night and the two following, Richelieu and the English troops attacked Fort Leon. They briefly captured it, but were driven out by a Spanish counterattack which cost the life of Miguel de Castana.

On the night of 19/20 June the garrison were briefly encouraged when a frigate from Ostend, loaded with ammunition, managed to slip through the English blockade. However on the same night the Compte de Soissons with his Swiss foot drove the Spaniards from their defences on the counterscarp. The Marquis de Leyde personally rallied the defenders, telling a wavering group of Italians that they would be more confident if, like him, they took off their armour. It was doubtful logic, quickly demonstrated when a few minutes later de Leyde was shot in the shoulder, and then injured in the face by an exploding grenade. The Spanish commander had himself carried into the town in an attempt to hide his injury from his men.

Fighting continued during the night of 20/21 June and in the morning Turenne sent in another summons to surrender. The defenders, ignorant of their commander's fall, said that they would await his orders. During the night of 21/22 June they sent out a number of the townspeople, and early on the 23rd requested a truce. Turenne leant that Major General de Bassecourt was now in command of the garrison, following the death of de Leyde early that morning. Terms were quickly agreed, and in the evening the Garde Française and some Swiss occupied part of the town.

The next day King Louis XIV arrived, greeted by a gun salute from the English fleet; on the 25th, as agreed in the surrender terms, the survivors of the Spanish garrison of Dunkirk, around 1,500 men, bringing with them two guns, marched out en route to St Omer. On the same day, following King Louis' ceremonial entry into Dunkirk, the town was as agreed handed over to Sir William Lockhart on behalf of Cromwell.

The English commander urged King Louis to spend the night in Dunkirk, but having ceremonially handed over the keys to the town, the French monarch preferred to retire to Mardyke. Though he appeared, for public consumption, to be content with the agreement, Louis preferred not to witness Dunkirk in English hands. Mazarin, outwardly at least, was more positive in his response, congratulating Cromwell on the fall of Dunkirk, despite the intrigues of those who had not favoured the Anglo-French alliance. He also felt that the destruction of the veteran Spanish foot in the recent battle meant that it would be a long time before the enemy would be in a position to take the offensive again.

Lockhart, however, reported to Thurloe that the ordinary French soldiers were enraged that 'so delicate a morsel' had been handed over to the English, and 'but for the efforts of Mazarin I am confident we should have been by the ears by now.'[1] Mazarin indeed faced a fair amount of criticism, particularly from elements of the clergy led by an old opponent, Cardinal de Retz, who argued that ceding Dunkirk and Mardyke not only strengthened Protestantism in Europe, but gave the English Republic a strategic foothold which it might one day use to attack France, which French soldiers had died to take. Mazarin remained unmoved. Until peace with Spain was concluded, he still needed English help.

In England news of the Battle of the Dunes, which reached London two days later, led to considerable official rejoicing; also a rather less than outstanding verse in homage to Cromwell, after his death, by the court poet Andrew Marvell:

> Astonished armies did their flight prepare.
> And cities strong were stormed by his prayer,
> Of that forever Preston's field shall tell
> The story and impregnable Clonmel,
> And where the sandy mountain Fenwick scaled,
> The sea between, yet hence his prayer prevailed.
> What man was ever so in Heaven obeyed
> Since the commanded sun on Gideon stayed?[2]

---

1   Birch, *Thurloe State Papers*, vol. vii, p.174.
2   Andrew Marvell, *Poem Upon the Death of his late Highness the Lord Protector*, lines 185–92.

THE FALL OF DUNKIRK

A national day of thanksgiving was ordered for 21 July. Meanwhile the campaign was resumed following the capture of Dunkirk.

Following the defeat at the Dunes, the Spanish forces had fallen back to Furnes. The Duke of York wrote that for some days afterwards:

> We thought our loss had been more considerable, than afterwards it proved; for most of our foot Officers, as well as our common Soldiers, got off, some by making their escape from the Enemy, others, and especially the officers, by giving small sums of money to those who had taken them, of which number was Don Antonio de Cordova, with many other Colonels and persons of note. So that by that time we came to Nieuport, which was about the 26th of the same month, all our Regiments of foot, excepting the King's and the natural Spaniards, were almost as strong as when they came into the field.[3]

When news of the fall of Dunkirk reached them, the Spanish commanders pulled back to Nieuport. A council of war was held, some officers proposing that that an attempt be made to hold the line of the canal between Nieuport and Dixmude. However the Duke of York opposed the suggestion, saying:

Andrew Marvell (1621–78).

> We had not sufficient strength of foot to maintain that post against a Victorious Army, ours being also disheartened by their late defeat. I also desired them to consider into what miserable condition we should be reduced, in case that pass should be forced upon us; for then it would be too late, and perhaps impossible to think of securing our great Towns, since the Enemy would have their choice of attacking, and also of mastering which of them they pleased, besides what other unknown mischiefs might arise from so hazardous an undertaking.[4]

The Duke proposed that the army should be divided among the garrisons of the towns in Western Flanders thought most likely to be attacked. By these means it was hoped that by the time the first one to be attacked fell, it would be too late for the enemy to attack any others. The Duke's plan was accepted, and he, with Caracena and 2,000 foot and the same number of horse, were to remain in Nieuport. A detachment under Condé were to go to Ostend. Don Juan with some foot and a large contingent of horse went to Bruges, and the rest under the Prince de Ligne to Ypres.

After the meeting Condé asked the Duke of York ' "Why would I venture to contradict Don Juan as I had done?" To which I answered him, "because I had no desire to be forced to run again, as we had done so lately at Dunkirk." '[5]

---

3   Sells, *Memoirs of James II*, p.275.
4   *Ibid.*
5   *Ibid.*, p.276.

'BETTER BEGGING THAN FIGHTING'

Nieuport.

James wrote that shortly after the other detachments left Nieuport, Turenne and the bulk of the French army reached Dixmude. The French vanguard came within cannon shot of Nieuport, but Turenne ordered a halt in operations as King Louis was 'desperately ill' in Calais. It was a lucky escape for the garrison, as that time they had only enough ammunition for less than 15 days. Fortunately the breathing space provided by Turenne enabled fresh supplies to be brought into Nieuport from Ostend, and work to be done on strengthening the defences.

Whilst the French army still remained inactive around Dixmude, the Spanish commanders held a meeting at Planquendal, on the Bruges–Nieuport Canal. Although it was impossible to muster a field army capable of meeting Turenne in open battle, it was decided that Don Juan, Caracena and Condé should muster at Bruges as many troops as could be spared from the garrisons, to shadow the movements of Turenne, who was now on the move again.

As agreed, 3,000 of the English foot were left to form the garrison of Dunkirk, while Major General Morgan, with his own regiment and those of Cochrane, Clarke and Lillingston would continue to campaign with the French army. The Spanish garrison of Bergues was invested on 27 June, and fell two days later, the allies taking 900 prisoners. There were some English casualties, including Lieutenant Colonel Richard Hughes, who was mortally wounded. Furnes, held by 80 men, fell on 3 July and Dixmude a few days later. The fortnight's pause which followed was partly, as the Duke of York claimed, because of the illness of King Louis, but also to give time to strengthen the defences of Dixmude.

Turenne's next objective was Gravelines, generally held to be the strongest place in Flanders. It had three ditches, filled each day by the tide, and a network of complex fortifications. The siege began at the end of July, operations being carried out by Marshal la Ferté with 10,000 men. Turenne,

THE FALL OF DUNKIRK

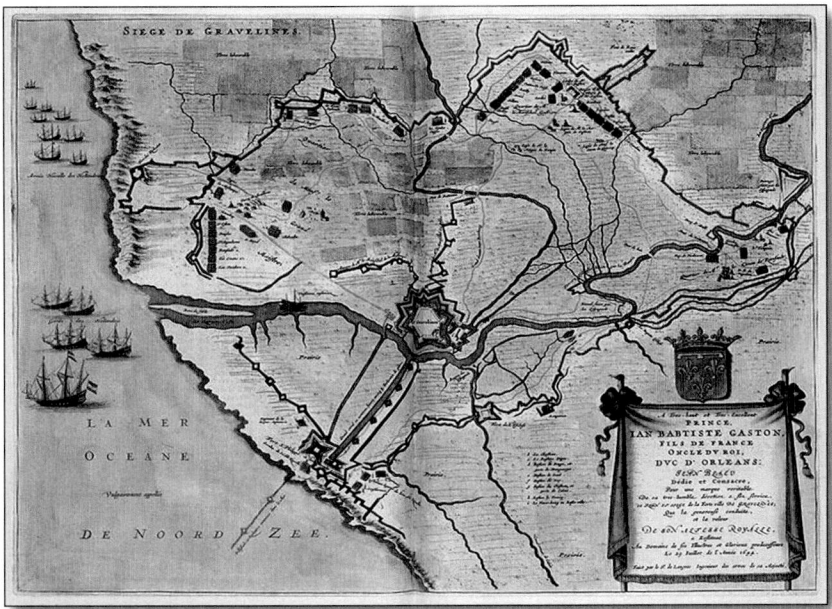

The Siege of Gravelines.

with 7,000 horse and 3,000 foot covered the siege and also stood ready to support the garrisons of Bergues, Furnes and Dixmude. English naval ships blockaded the harbour.

The scratch force which Don Juan and Condé had put together made a half-hearted relief attempt, reaching St Omer before Turenne blocked their advance. Gravelines surrendered on 27 August. On 9 September marching from Ypres to Tournai with 3,500 men, Turenne took Oudenarde by surprise after a night march. Some parties of French cavalry came within four leagues of Brussels. Turenne felt that if he had had heavy guns and fresh men, he could have taken the city. On 13 September, the same day that Cromwell died, the Prince de Ligne, who had been marching from Ypres to Tournai, was intercepted by Turenne and routed with the loss of most of his men. The Duke of York felt this was a worse defeat than the Battle of the Dunes, as there was now nothing to prevent the allies from occupying more towns. Menin quickly surrendered, and then the allies moved on Ypres. Situated in the middle of a marsh, which rendered access difficult, and held by 800 foot and 500 horse, Ypres might have been expected to put up prolonged resistance, but surrendered on 26 September.

It was the end of the campaign, and for all practical purposes, of the war.

9

Aftermath

The winter of 1658–9 was a time of considerable hardship for what remained on the Royalist army of Charles II. Some of the officers were still prisoners in Paris, and remained in custody until peace seemed likely between France and Spain. They were set free on 21 June 1659, having pledged to surrender themselves if hostilities were resumed. They had no clothes other than those they had been captured in, and were being pursued and threatened with imprisonment by various creditors.

Those men, about 2,000 in all, still with the colours in Flanders received little support. Pay was small and frequently in arrears, and after a truce was signed with France, the Spaniards had no interest in assisting them. John Gwynne described the hardships of this time:

Some of my soldiers one morning came to me grievously sharp set, and in that hungry humour sadly complained of the hard measure they had, as to be forced to beg, steal, or starve, which was not always to be done, nor would they do it any longer; vowing that it was for my sake they stayed there too long languishing at that rate. I could not take anything ill that eased them with talking, because, to be sure, whatsoever they begged, stole, or made a shift for, I had my share of it, or I might have gone and do as they did, or not live. Therefore I seemed to comply with them to gain their patience but to the next day. And, in the meantime, I would fix upon something commendable for us all to do in so great an exigence, and so prevailed with them.[1]

Gwynne addressed his men again next day, reminding them that he had endured similar circumstances:

You all know very well that not long since I was in quarters, with Colonel Carles his lieutenant, and others, and truly we had no other choice for our Christmas Day dinner than a well-grown young fat dog, as cleanly dressed and as finely roasted, as any man need put into his belly. And we had no need to complain, since we had anything to feed upon as was man's meat. Nor need you want such novelty now and then, if you do but look well about you when you go abroad a-preying, whilst there is a care taken for a better accommodation for us. In the meantime,

---

1 Tucker and Young, Gwynne's *Military Memoirs, op. cit.*

let's all resolve, with a brave old saying, 'What cannot be cured, must be endured.' For we come here to live and die in the King's service without scrupling. But, like gentlemen and soldiers,

We'll here in point of honour starve, and try
How long we'll pine with hunger ere we die.[2]

Once stragglers had returned after the battle of the Dunes, the Royalist army probably had around 2,000 effective foot. On 11 September Lord Newburgh reported that the Duke of York was at Bruges with 1,000 foot and 500 horse.

During the winter and spring of 1658/9 the Royalist forces were reorganised. The death of Oliver Cromwell in the previous September had raised Royalist hopes for a change in the political atmosphere in Britain, with renewed plans for a general insurrection. It was important that a body of troops should be ready to land in support of such a rising. The reorganisation was not achieved without recriminations. The Earl of Bristol lost his regiment to the Duke of York, and complained bitterly. After Bristol refused it, the Duke of Gloucester's Regiment was given to an Irish officer, Colonel Fitzpatrick – 'a coxcomb'. The lieutenant colonel of York's Regiment was made Lieutenant Colonel of a regiment of horse which it was planned to raise.[3]

By July 1659 the Royalist army consisted once more, in theory at least, of six regiments: the King's Regiment of Foot, the Duke of York's, Colonel Fitzpatrick's, Lord Newburgh's, Colonel Grace's and Colonel Farrell's. The largest was the Duke of York's with 19 companies, the smallest Lord Newburgh's with ten. In all there were 86 companies, totalling between 2,000–3,000 men.

In August news arrived of the Royalist rising in England headed by Sir George Booth. This seemed to be the opportunity for which the Royalists had been waiting. But the end of hostilities between France and Spain complicated matters. In a shift in policy, Turenne offered his old comrade in arms the Duke of York, ships, munitions and supplies, and even 2,000 French troops. He urged that the Royalist forces march to Boulogne, where ships would be waiting. However Caracena, Governor of the Spanish Netherlands, proved uncooperative. As James discovered:

> Notwithstanding the Duke of Gloucester had delivered to the Marquis of Caracena the letters which Duke his Royal Highness had written from Boulogne for the marching of his troops to St Omer, yet the marquis would not permit them to stir out of their quarters, though he was sufficiently pressed to it by the Duke of Gloucester. But he still answered, he did not believe Mr de Turenne durst let them pass through any part of his King's dominions without order, which he knew he could not have. Nor would he suffer to draw down to the sea side, to which he

---

2   *Ibid.*, pp.132–3.
3   Macray, *Calendar of the Clarendon State Papers*, vol. 4, p.39.

was also urged by the Duke of Gloucester, when he found he could not obtain his first point.[4]

Although a number of French officers supported Turenne, Mazarin was not willing to support open action against the English Republic until peace between France and Spain was finalised in November by the Treaty of the Pyrenees. The Spanish were unwilling to incur further hostile attention from the English government by giving active support to the Royalists.

It was the effective end of the Royalist army in exile as a fighting force. It would remain scattered in various Flanders garrisons until the Restoration of Charles II to the English throne in May 1660.

Meanwhile, as the final actions of the Franco-Spanish war in Flanders were being played out, it had fallen to Sir William Lockhart to take charge of England's new possessions of Dunkirk and Mardyke. He estimated that in order to hold them securely against Spanish (or perhaps French) attempts to take them, Mardyke needed a garrison of 1,000 foot, Dunkirk about 2,500 foot and 500 horse, and Fort Royal, an outpost on the road to Bergues, 500 foot. He never in fact had more than 3,000 men in all. 'There will be need of 5 or 6 good troops of horse. I mean strong, at least 70 in a troop, and it's no matter, whether they be single troops or a regiment, for the commander in chief of the whole forces will often have use for them, in parties, but seldom in a body.' They should have carbines to add to their usual equipment: 'Carbines, and good ones, and very needful to them, for we must march for the most part betwixt dykes and water gauges, and will many times be put to use their carbines when their pistols would be useless.' Without cavalry, the route between Mardyke and Dunkirk would be vulnerable to enemy raiders. Indeed four horses had just been carried off from near Mardyke by a party from Gravelines.[5]

Lockhart requested that each troops should include 10 veteran soldiers drafted from other units, but as most cavalry troops were below strength Parliament preferred to raise entirely new troops.

Lockhart's own troop landed at Dunkirk early in August, those of Captains Nicholas and Flower early in September Captain Broadnax's on 25 July. In August Tobias Bridge was appointed Major. Captain Flower had distinguished himself at the siege of Dunkirk and the battle of the Dunes. Broadnax, however, did not impress Lockhart: 'He is a pretty man, but if I may speak my thought of humour of the experience of one converse he seems to promise no extraordinary matter.' He had brought his men to Flanders unarmed, and in August his 'incapable lieutenant neglecting orders' allowed his men to be surprised whilst foraging. Five troopers were lost and 10 horses. Once the regiment was complete, Lockhart took personal command, and in September mounted raids which captured 500 cattle and 30–40 horses from the Nieuport garrison. A week later 1,000 cattle were brought in from the villages around St Omer.[6]

---

4   Sells, *Memoirs of James II*, p.275.
5   Birch, *Thurloe State Papers*, vol. vii, pp.170, 215, 260, 288–9.
6   *Mercurius Politicus*, no. 433, 9–16 September 1658, p.822.

At this stage the garrison consisted of Lockhart's regiment, Alsop's, nine companies of Colonel Gibbon's and nine of Colonel Salmon's. The last two were officially part of the English establishment, not of the Flanders contingent. He also had a regiment of horse under Colonel Bridges, and in August half of Lillington's regiment of foot was quartered at Mardyke.

As long as hostilities continued, Turenne's army and neighbouring French garrisons bolstered the security of the English possessions, and the Spanish in any case had no field army capable of offensive operations. This was fortunate, as the defences of Dunkirk had been badly damaged during the siege, and at Mardyke constant work was needed to keep the defensive ditches clear of drifting sand. Lockhart claimed that the Dunkirk defences had been repaired by the end of August, though in the following May Colonel Alsop said that it would be impossible to hold the town in the event of serious attack, and that Mardyke could only be held for four days.

It was clear from the start that England's new possessions would be expensive to maintain. They would never cost less than £60,000–£70,000 per year, and in time of war probably much more. Some funds could be obtained from local taxes and customs revenues, and, as long as the war continued, nearby Spanish-held villages could be raided. However French troops were competing for these resources, which were scanty in any case, and this resulted in constant friction between the allies. Lockhart indeed saw the surrounding countryside as a source of fodder and provisions. He proposed that one month's supply of biscuit should always be kept in store as emergency provisions for the garrison. In April 1659 it was estimated that the pay of the three regiments of foot and one of horse forming the Dunkirk garrison would be £77,366 a year, together with the cost of clothing. Dunkirk's own income from local taxation and excise duties was around £21,000 per year.

So far as relations with the civilian population of Dunkirk were concerned, the main difficulties which arose were with regard to religion. Before the French had granted possession of Dunkirk to England, Lockhart had to sign a declaration agreeing to preserve the rights and freedom of worship to Catholics in the town. Lockhart was content to accept this, but opposed any attempts to extend the rights of the townspeople. After some argument, Mazarin accepted the inevitable 'and acknowledged that his Highness had the only title to all that can be claimed of jurisdiction over the town as prince and sovereign, and that he alone hath right to all the powers, profits and emoluments that were due to any of their former princes.' The inhabitants had been promised the enjoyment of their property, religious toleration and justice according to their usual laws and customs, and that was all that Cromwell was prepared to grant.[7]

Lockhart's first task, apart from the repair of Dunkirk's defences, was to ensure the discipline and good behaviour of the troops. The citizens on the whole bowed to the inevitable, and even claimed that they had wished in any case to come under English rule, provided their freedom of worship was

---

7   Birch, *Thurloe State Papers*, vol. viii, p.125.

permitted. Lockhart, probably with good reason, did not entirely believe these assurances, and imposed an oath, by which all inhabitants were to swear allegiance to Cromwell and his successors, and to report any conspiracies they became aware of. They were also all disarmed. Those who wished to remain under Spanish rule were permitted to leave. Lockhart explained 'I have given them leave to transport their goods to Nieuport as peaceably as if they had removed from one street in London to another.'[8]

The most pressing problem for Lockhart was the attitude of his troops towards the Catholic region. Orders were issued threatening severe punishment to any soldier who might 'offer injury or abuse to the ecclesiastics or Romish churchmen of what order soever, or condition, in the streets, in their houses, convents or churches.' The religious views of the soldiers was an ongoing problem. As soon as they occupied Dunkirk 'it was openly discoursed among them that it was fit to pillage the place, and especially the churches where there was much riches.' The irreverence of the soldiers was demonstrated and 'went to the height that one of them lighted his pipe of tobacco at one of the wax candles of the altar where the priest was saying mass.' The soldiers were told that if they had to go into the Catholic churches to satisfy their curiosity, 'it was fit to come so as they should not give disturbance to others in that which they imagined to be their devotion.'[9]

There were about 50 nuns in Dunkirk, who were contracted to help take care of sick and wounded soldiers. The friars and other clergy in the town protested about the clause in the oath imposed by Lockhart requiring disclosure of any plots they heard of. They argued that anything revealed in the confessional must remain confidential, and it is unclear how or if the difficulty was ever resolved. Lockhart remained pessimistic about relations with the clergy:

> The ecclesiastics here find so little of that ill treatment which the Spaniards threatened them with, as they pretend that they are well satisfied with us, and say we use them better than either the Spaniards or French did, which probably is true. But all that's done for them is like washing of the blackamoor, for their hearts cannot be gained; and what is done for them is rather to satisfy others than out of any hopes to do good upon them.

His hope was that the clergy would eventually succumb to Spanish pressure, and leave the town. Alternatively they might become involved in conspiracies of some kind, and give Lockhart the excuse to expel them.[10]

Lockhart hoped that the Catholic presence would steadily diminish, and that Dunkirk could be populated by English or European settlers. 'If any English family will transport themselves here, provided they bring with them a line from my lord Thurloe, mentioning their fidelity and affection to your highness's government, I shall see them settled and serve them faithfully'. French Huguenots showed interest, but this seemed likely to cause problems

---

8   *Ibid.*, vol. vii, p.197.
9   *Ibid.*, p.223.
10 *Ibid.*, p.249.

with the French government, so Lockhart preferred to encourage Protestants from Flanders. He felt that a subscription should be mounted in England to provide assistance to Flemish Protestants hoping to move to Dunkirk to escape Spanish persecution.[11]

One problem was the lack of a Protestant church in Dunkirk. The only existing church was Catholic, and Lockhart resisted pressure to commandeer it for Protestant use. Instead he took over the market hall, though there was a shortage of Protestant clergy in Flanders. There were no regimental chaplains, and even Lockhart's own chaplain was ordered home. Lockhart felt that ministers of particular ability were needed to win the population over from Catholicism, and in reply the famous, or infamous, Hugh Peters, Chaplain to the army was sent over, but was not, according to Lockhart, an unqualified success. Peters was a notorious agitator, and Lockhart complained that 'if it were possible to get him to mind preaching, and to forbear troubling himself with other things, he would certainly be a fit minster for the soldiers.'[12] Peters showed signs of wanting to stay in Dunkirk if requested, but Lockhart made sure that no such request materialised. Despite the low-key approach of the new administration there were changes at Dunkirk. The images of the Virgin Mary over the gates were replaced with the arms of the Lord Protector, the Sabbath was to be observed strictly, and penalties for non-observance of Saints Days were abolished. Lockhart, rather complacently, told Thurloe: 'Your lordship would have admired to see the posture this town was in the last lords day, not a shop open not anything indecent that was to be seen.' There were of course complaints and grumbling from priests and others, but the townspeople as a whole seemed accepting. Lockhart told Thurloe: 'The temper of the generality of the people here is docile and tractable. I am confident a hundred French would be more unquiet and unmanageable than the whole body of this town.'[13]

There were indeed hopes that English territory could be expanded with the capture of Ostend, but negotiations with Mazarin to help bring this about were frustrated by the death of Cromwell on 3 September 1658. Mardyke and Dunkirk would remain as the sole English prizes from the war in Flanders.

The Dunkirk garrison was generally under-strength, particularly whilst active campaigning was still continuing, with Lockhart having to send drafts of men to replace losses in those units serving with Turenne's force. Eventually Turenne was persuaded to send half of Lillingston's regiment to reinforce the Dunkirk garrison.

Richard Cromwell was accepted in Dunkirk as his father's successor without difficulty, and Lockhart sent back to Paris to act as English ambassador, though the French ambassador in London feared that his departure might make Dunkirk more vulnerable to being taken by the Spanish through treachery or surprise attack. It was not a concern shared by the English government, and at the end of 1659 all but two companies of Salmon and Gibbons regiments were withdrawn to England, although 400 old soldiers

---

11 *Ibid.*, p.205.
12 *Ibid.*
13 *Ibid.*, p.249.

from the English establishment were promised as replacements. Lockhart was also told to ask for the return of the remaining half of Lillingston's Regiment. This was agreed and it was despatched by sea from Calais, though half were drowned when their ship was wrecked. George Monck reported on 3 February that Lockhart had ordered five companies of the regiment under Major Mallory to march to the coast and take shipping at St Valery. 'But the said vessels by reason of a tempest were separated, and the one vessel got safe to Dunkirk but the other, wherein was the Major, and divers officers with two companies and a half, had been missed seven days when my letters were dated, which caused great doubt that they are shipwrecked.'[14]

Control of the garrison was in the hands of Colonels Alsop and Lillingston, and it was noted that the defences had greatly decayed owing to lack of funds to maintain them. However the truce agreed between France and Spain on April 28 1659, which included Dunkirk, removed any realistic danger of a Spanish attempt to regain the town. The outbreak of Booth's Rising in the summer of 1659 led to the recall to England in August of the Regiments of Cochrane, Morgan and Clarke. Not all were classed as part of the Dunkirk garrison, but Colonels Alsop and Lillingston, who clearly disliked Cochrane, complained that he 'carried away near 200 of our soldiers,' despite his officers promising that they would not do so. But 'indeed it could not be well prevented by us, by reason of their being shipped by night; but by information of some of our officers we hear that many of our soldiers were disguised (in their clothes etc, without red coats) by some officers of those regiments, on purpose to deceive us.'[15]

This, the colonels said, left them with no more than 2,500 foot, 'which is a very weak garrison for this place with its forts.'[16] Without 3,000 men they could not promise to hold out if besieged. Cochrane's Regiment would eventually mutiny in England after its colonel was cashiered and six companies were ordered to return to Flanders. The regiment was disbanded in February 1660, though some of its men were probably used to fill out some of the units in Flanders.

Political changes in England led to the Parliament ordering in the early summer of 1659 seven commissioners to purge the army of politically suspect or 'immoral' officers. The Dunkirk garrison did not fare well in the investigation. 'Here does want a person to command the garrison whose principle it is to encourage godliness in the power thereof. We have cause to fear that profanes and wickedness, (which do sadly abound in this place) will do more to the loss and prejudice whereof than all other enemies.' Other complaints, possibly from rival colleagues, were more specific. Alsop was admitted to be an 'active man as a soldier, but an enemy to religion and godliness, especially in the sincerity of it.' Lillington 'a mere soldier, who thinketh religion altogether useless in military discipline, or he would not cherish such a crew of wicked officers as he doth.' Of Alsop's officers, it was said: 'There are not above six commission officers in this regiment but are

---

14　Firth, *The Clarke Papers*, vol. III, pp.179–80.
15　Birch, *Thurloe State Papers*, vol. vii, pp.722–3.
16　*Ibid.*

guilty of whoring, swearing or drinking, besides false musters.' Lockhart's own regiment fared no better.[17]

Lillington and Alsop complained vigorously to the Council of State:

> We cannot conceal the great regret we have to understand, that divers officers here, by some unworthy persons, have been traduced to your honours, though we know them to be men that have all along served you faithfully and cordially. We cannot believe that your honours will be ready to believe detractors, but rather to credit our testimony; for we assure you, that if we did conceive or suspect any officer of this garrison not fit for his command, either in respect of his fidelity or conversation, we should be most ready, according to our duty, to inform your honours. But truly we believe there are not in all your armies men that have demeaned themselves with more fidelity, courage and honesty, both in England and here, wherein those that backbite them have been wanting too apparently.[18]

Hugh Peters (1598–1660).

There seems nothing to suggest that the colonels and their men were particularly different in their behaviour from other units of the army. Alsop and Lillingston were competent professional soldiers, who performed effectively despite the problems which they faced in dealing with authorities in England which often neglected their needs:

> If we have not these supplies and the other necessaries, we cannot answer what you may perhaps expect of us, though we perish in the defence of this place, which our ambition and desire is to perpetuate to our nation, as a goad in the sides of their enemies, and to secure our footing in the Continent of Europe, lost since Queen Mary's days, and now regained; and doubtless we ought to preserve that carefully, which the Lord hath given us so graciously.[19]

Lockhart resumed command at the end of 1659, and stayed true to his trust in the politically tumultuous opening months of 1660, despite attempts by Royalists and French to bribe or persuade him to hand over Dunkirk to them. By the spring he and most of his men felt that the restoration of Charles II was the only way in which to maintain order and stability in England. On 1 April Samuel Pepys noted that it was reported that 'the soldiers at Dunkirk

---

17 C. H. Firth and Godfrey Davies, *The Regimental History of Cromwell's Army*, vol. II (Oxford: Clarendon Press, 1940), pp.112–3.
18 *Ibid.*
19 *Ibid.*, p.114.

'BETTER BEGGING THAN FIGHTING'

Edward Harley (1624-1700).

do drink the King's health in the streets.'[20] On 8 May Colonel Lillingston presented to General George Monck an address from the garrison pledging their full support for the King's return.

Although Sir William Lockhart had not opposed the Restoration, it was hardly likely that he would retain his command. One of the first acts of King Charles II was to replace him with Colonel Edward Harley, apparently because of fears that Lockhart might hand Dunkirk over to the French. Harley, from a Herefordshire Parliamentarian family, had commanded a regiment of foot in the New Model Army between 1645–47, and was an MP for Herefordshire. He was commissioned as Governor of Dunkirk on 14 July 1660, and took over Sir William Lockhart's Regiment of Foot. Sir William's Regiment of horse was given to Lockhart's brother, Robert. Alsop and Lillingston were retained for the moment, although their regiments were purged of officers whose loyalty was suspect.

Parliament had passed an act annexing Dunkirk in perpetuity to the English crown, so the need to retain a garrison meant that the regiments there were not disbanded with the bulk of the army in the autumn of 1660. It was decided that a garrison of 3,600 foot and 432 horse (one regiment) were needed. The question was how this force should be raised, and the government saw in Dunkirk the opportunity to employ some troops whose presence in mainland Britain might well be politically embarrassing. In Flanders already were the former soldiers of the Republic who formed the present garrison, and the remains of the King's army in exile. It was decided to amalgamate the two to form the Dunkirk garrison.

The Royalist troops were still more neglected at the Restoration, for the Spanish authorities now regarded them as King Charles' responsibility, and petitions from their officers for assistance grew increasingly desperate. The officers of the King's Regiment, then quartered at Nivelles, sent a desperate plea that:

> We are scarcely left one part in four who at Dunkirk battle entirely devoted themselves to be sacrificed for our king's sake, rather than deceive his reposed confidence in the resolve of his too few (at that time) loyal subjects. But having escaped the worst, beyond our hope, as to be prisoners, three parts of us perished with a tedious imprisonment, and want of bread, and the few remainder here languish as having no allowance to live.[21]

---

20 *Samuel Pepys Diary* (ed. Wheatley) p.104.
21 Gwynne, *Military Memoirs*, p.127.

They had received no reply by the end of 1660, and were moved to Namur for the winter. Caracena, who clearly regarded them as a nuisance, instructed the town authorities that they were to be given no accommodation other than 'vacant houses upon the ramparts and courts of guard (presumably unoccupied barrack huts) and to expect their own subsistence from their own King, being restored to three kingdoms.'[22]

After further pleas from their officers, in March 1661 they were ordered to march to Dunkirk, and between March and October reorganised and re-equipped there. Interestingly, in view of their former armament, in June 1662 the Regiment of Guards was to be re-armed with 400 pikes, 300 muskets and 300 firelocks. On 22 July Colonel Will Legge, Master of the Ordnance, was issued a warrant for '£976 13s 4d, to issue the kings guards at Dunkirk with 800 bandoliers and 1,200 sword belts.'[23] The King's Regiment was now regarded as part of the garrison, and possibly because they were English and not Irish, seem to have been on good terms with the former Commonwealth troops there.

Lord Rutherford was now Governor, and as described in a newssheet account of June 1661, 'hath viewed and examined all the stores, tried the granadoes etc, and upon a strict survey of the officers and soldiers, finds them twixt 6 and 7,000 men effective; all stout and experienced soldiers, as their neighbours can testify.'[24] A week later it was reported that 'His Majesty's Regiment here is almost fully completed, consisting of twelve companies, and in each company one hundred men.'[25]

Rutherford also took steps to quarter the troops in 'several cantons' of the town, 'to lodge the soldiery appropriately.'[26]

On 22 August Rutherford reported to Secretary Nicholas that 'The spirits of the garrison are not rectified; they need alloying with others or there must be great change of officers, enclosing a list of officers who must be replaced.'[27]

By September work was underway on repairing the outworks, and construction of 'the great fort', protecting the harbour, begun. Storm damage in November allegedly resulted in the officers and men of the King's Regiment petitioning Rutherford that 'they might have some work to do for his Majesty's service, which employment they would willingly undertake gratis, to express their thankfulness for his special care of that garrison.'[28] It was claimed that their example was quickly followed by the officers of the other regiments of the garrison. Work was supervised by the royal Engineer General, Sir Bernard de Gomme and 'Mr Jessin' engineer to the garrison, 'a most laborious and ingenenious person.'[29]

Probably with a degree of exaggeration, the newspaper account went on: 'T'was pleasant to see the commanders and officers march at the head of

---

22 Ibid.
23 M. A. E. Green (ed.), *Calendar of State Papers, Domestic Series, of the reign of Charles II. 1660–1661* (London: Longman, et al., 1860), p.332.
24 Ibid., pp.8, 41, 409.
25 Scott, *History of the British Army*, III, pp.117–8.
26 *Mercurius Publicus*, no. 124, June 20–27 1661, p.386.
27 Firth, 'Royalist and Cromwellian Armies in Flanders', p.116.
28 *Mercurius Publicus*, no. 157, September 7–14 1661, p.402.
29 Ibid.

their companies, with drums beating and every one of them a shovel on his shoulder, and their soldiers expressing great cheerfulness in their expression, by dancing to the work.'[30]

During the winter of 1661–62, the remaining royalist units were reorganised, and a number of supernumerary officers dismissed.

The Duke of York's Regiment, commanded by Lord Muskerry, another strong unit of around 1,000 men, was also placed on the establishment of the garrison, but, perhaps because the troops were mainly Irish, it was not brought into the town. Instead it was quartered at Mardyke, where a traveller in May 1662 saw them: 'I was at Mardyke, the houses whereof being burnt down I saw not above six standing. A regiment of Irish, being the Duke of York's, keep a camp there, in huts made of sod.'[31] In June 1661, the Privy Seal granted £7,000 as two month's pay for the regiment.

Also something of an embarrassment was the Regiment of Lord Taaffe, formerly commanded by the Duke of Gloucester, who had died in September 1660. This unit was almost entirely neglected, and left at Mardyke. A number of officers were dismissed in the winter of 1661–2, and in December of 1661, pay warrants were issued for 500 officers and men, although the real total was probably much less.

In the spring of 1661 all the Irish regiments including those of Richard Grace and Colonel Farrell, along with the Scottish regiment of Lord Newburgh, in all about 1,700–1,800 men, were at Mardyke.

Sir Edward Harley had considered moving them nearer to Dunkirk, but as he told the Duke of Albermarle, their officers felt that except in an emergency 'their troops will be much incommoded when they shall be in so narrow a room as they must be if they remove under the town walls, for although there are not in the troops above 1600 effective men, yet there are many more women and children, who take up much room.'[32] Harley felt that:

> The troops will be of more service at Mardyke to countenance the new works upon Fort Lyon side, and if the Spaniards will attempt to fall upon the Irish at Mardyke, then it is much more likely that the Spaniards will possess Mardyke, and make a quarter there; besides I must freely acquaint your Grace, that I very much doubt when the Irish and English come so near together they will not agree so well as at this distance.[33]

There were periodic rumours of potentially hostile Spanish troop movements, though nothing came of them.

Garrison duty in Flanders was never popular and officers in particular had a tendency to award themselves leave. On 30 December all absent officers were ordered to repair to Dunkirk within 10 days, or face dismissal. Those

---

30 *Ibid.*
31 Historical Manuscripts Commission, Popham MSS, London, 1902; M. A. E. Green (ed.), *Calendar of State Papers, Domestic Series, of the reign of Charles II. 1661-1662* (London: Longman et al., 1861), p.288
32 *Ibid.*
33 *Ibid.*

listed included Sir Anthony Cope of Falkland's Regiment and a number of other officers from that and the King's Regiments. On the same day Secretary Nicholas urged Lord Rutherford to be sparing in using licenses for officers to go to England and not to issue any covering longer than one month: 'He is to suppress the drunkenness and debauchery which are practiced at Dunkirk, to the scandal of the nation, and to send to the King the names of such officers who not forbear on admonition, and they will be cashiered.'[34]

The reform of the old Royalist regiments caused a good deal of discontent. On 21 June Captain Edmund Fitzgerald of the Duke of Gloucester's Regiment petitioned for a payment of 300 guilders promised by the Duke in consideration of his dismissal from the regiment. He had also served in the Duke of York's Regiment, and asked for some place in the Horse Guards.[35]

In February 1662 the Irish officers 'lately disbanded at Mardyke', and also Lord Newburgh's Scots, petitioned the King for subsistence. They had 'repaired to him in Flanders from foreign parts in 1656, leaving advantageous employment. Since the restoration their case had been much harder than those of others of the king's officers.'[36]

In February there was a further petition from the officers of the Duke of York's Regiment. They received a verbal assurance 'of His Majesty's care, but they have attended long, and pawned and sold all they had, even their very clothes and arms, to maintain themselves.'[37]

On 27 February a warrant was issued authorising to pay to Lord Newburgh and Colonels Grace, Farrell and Geraldine (Fitzgerald) the sums due to their regiments for 14 days' pay prior to the reformation of the Dunkirk garrison

In March it was somewhat optimistically laid down that the regiments of the Dunkirk garrison should each have an establishment of 10 companies with 100 men each. The Duke of York's Regiment was to have an establishment of 12 companies, although it was tacitly acknowledged that this establishment would not be reached when it was agreed that the regiment should receive pay for 1,200 men, with the excess to be spent on beds and bedding.[38]

During the summer preparations got under way for transporting the King's Regiment of Foot back to England. On 22 August orders were given for Captain Walters' company to be shipped to Guernsey, and Captains Sydenham and Jeffries to Jersey. In September a warrant was issued to Colonel Lord Wentworth for Captain Morley's company to be shipped to Plymouth, complete with beds and bedding. And when on 4 November Lord Rutherford handed Dunkirk over to the French, the rest of the Guards were to be transported to England to be distributed among garrisons there. The Duke of York's Regiment was to be transferred to French service. Apparently it was disbanded a couple of years later. Three troops of horse, Lord Rutherford's and Lord Falkland's Regiments and the 'train' and staff were to be disbanded before 17 November, if possible:

---

34 Green, *CSPD Charles II., 1660–1*, p.543.
35 Green, *CSPD Charles II., 1661–2*, p.198.
36 *Ibid.*, p.222.
37 *Ibid.*, p.225.
38 *Ibid.*, p.301.

The arms of the disbanded troops are to be given up, the magazines of bread and cheese distributed among the soldiers, unless otherwise required, and the town delivered according to instructions, keeping only a sufficient number of soldiers for security, till the money has been received and embarked. Vessels are to be hired for the men to return. They are to have passes to their respective towns, and to be ordered to sell their swords and horses within 14 days of their arrival.[39]

On 4 November it was ordered that the three remaining companies of the King's Guards were to be landed at Deal. And on 28 November, in a distinct afterthought, at the request of Rutherford an order was sent to Colonel Lord Taafe to disband the former regiment of the Duke of Gloucester.[40]

It gradually became clear, however, to the government in London that Dunkirk was both costly to maintain, and probably indefensible in the event of a determined siege by in particular the French, so in November 1662, Lord Rutherford found himself dealing with negotiations to sell Dunkirk to France. This was rendered easier by King Charles' acquisition of Tangiers as part of the dowry of his Portuguese queen, Catherine of Braganza. The need to garrison this inhospitable new acquisition against the constant attacks by the Moors, provided an ideal solution for what to do with the politically embarrassing and in some cases suspect troops at Dunkirk.

The King's Regiment of Foot was much more acceptable because of its predominantly English composition. It was shipped back to England, and incorporated with the Kings' Regiment of Foot Guards. The Irish and Scottish troops were a more difficult problem. The officers of the Irish regiments commented that, as former rebels, their men, 'in spite of their fidelity, fear that if they return to Ireland, their arms will be taken from them, and they thrown into goal, on pretence of dangerousness.'[41] The Duke of York's Regiment, as the strongest and most viable unit, was disposed of on the cessation of Dunkirk by being returned to French service. It was evidently disbanded a couple of years later. The remnants of the other regiments, in Richard Grace's case only 80 men, were amalgamated and incorporated in the units sent to garrison Tangier. Farrell's Regiment, probably originally the Earl of Bristol's, was shipped to Tangiers in November 1661, totaling 381 men when it arrived. Fitzgerald's reached Mardyke from Beauvais in March 1661, and had 395 men when it arrived in Tangiers.[42]

Lord Newburgh's Scots had been quartered at Douai in December 1660, the officers complaining that they were starving, having sold or pawned all they had. They had had no rations of bread for six months and except for five florins, no pay. They were moved to Mardyke in the spring of 1661, reduced to two companies and evidently incorporated into an Irish regiment.[43]

In May 1660 there were four Cromwellian regiments in the Dunkirk garrison. In May 1661, when Lord Rutherford became governor, he took over the regiment formerly commanded by Lockhart then Harley. This

---

39 *Ibid.*, p.386.
40 *Ibid.*, pp.8, 41, 409.
41 *Ibid.*, p.281.
42 Firth and Davies, *The Regimental History of Cromwell's Army*, vol. II, p.167.
43 *Ibid.*, p.118.

AFTERMATH

Tangiers under English occupation.

unit was disbanded after Dunkirk was sold to the French, although some of the officers then served in the Tangiers garrison. Rutherford, who had been created Earl of Teviot, became the first Governor of Tangier, but was killed in an action with the Moors on 4 May 1664. Major Knightley of his old Dunkirk regiment died with him. Another of the regiment's officers, Lieutenant Colonel Henry Norwood, became Deputy Governor of Tangiers.

Lillingston's regiment had passed to Robert Harley, Sir Edward's brother, and with 947 men was sent to Tangiers in January 1662. The then governor, the Earl of Peterborough, wrote to Harley that 'You have here come under my inspection, a regiment of the most estimable I have known, and that is governed by sober, able and discreet officers.' It bore the brunt of fighting for the next year, losing around 400 men, and in October 1663 was reduced into the governor's Regiment.[44]

Alsop's Regiment was on the Restoration given first to Lord Ossory, and then to Lord Falkland. Many of the officers were demoted or replaced by Royalists. The regiment was disbanded in November 1661, but the redoubtable Alsop had a long and distinguished career at Tangiers, serving as joint governor in 1676, and receiving a medal from the King in appreciation of his loyalty.

Three troops of what had been Lockhart's regiment of Horse were sent in April 1662 as part of the English contingent assisting the Portuguese against Spain. The remainder were disbanded in November 1662, though Major Tobias Bridge at least, saw service in Tangiers.

They were not the first nor last of the servants of the House of Stuart to experience the ingratitude of kings.

---

44 *Ibid.*, p.105.

Colour Plate Commentaries

Plate C

5: Commonwealth infantry, 1658 campaign

The Alliance formed between the Commonwealth and France called for the creation of a corps of some six thousand men to serve in Flanders. The expense of raising and arming these men was to be met jointly between England and France.

The expeditionary force was to be organised into six infantry regiments, each of a thousand men, organised into two five company battalions. The bulk of the men raised were volunteers based around a kernel of veterans.

The force consisting entirely of infantry was under the command of Sir John Reynolds, with Major General Thomas Morgan as second in command. Whilst it was dressed in the standard red coat of the New Model Army; their armament however differed from the rest of the army which provided each regiment with a 1 pike to 2 musket ratio in that the numbers of pikes and muskets were equal. Armour was also issued. The retrograde musket to pike ratio and issuing of full set of armour was at French request.

Plate D

6: Royalist Musketeer

The alliance agreed between Cromwell and Mazarin forced the exiled the English Royalists to leave France and to seek refuge with King Philip IV of Spain. The exiled Stuart king, Charles II, set up his headquarters in Bruges; however, the limitation of Spanish funds provided barely enough to form five regiments of foot (later six) and two troops of horse.

This musketeer belongs to the King's Own Regiment of Guards, often referred to as Wentworth's Regiment of Guards. The regiment was formed from the merger of a Guards regiment raised by Henry Wilmot, the Earl of Rochester and another similar raised by Lord Wentworth. According to James II the regiment fielded some 400 at the start of the 1658 campaign. When it returned to England in 1662, it was recorded as clothed in red, however as it was raised in Spanish service, it is possible that it was originally clothed in grey wool. A fabric popular in the Spanish army.

COLOUR PLATE COMMENTARIES

Plate E

7: Royalist trooper or junior officer of horse in the Lifeguard of the Duke of York.

Raised as a personal bodyguard to the Duke of York in 1655 and commanded by Sir Charles Berkeley. The Lifeguards, which charged several times with the Duke himself at their head, suffered severely but remained fit for further service. James was to state that the troop numbered some 50 troopers in 1658.

8: Buff coat
The trooper's buff coat in illustration 7 is composed of four large pieces and sleeves, and is based on this surviving example found in the collection of Shropshire Museum Service. It is on display at the Music Hall Museum, Shrewsbury.

Bibliography

Primary Sources

Birch, Thomes (ed.), Thurloe, John, *A Collection of the State Papers of John Thurloe*, 7 vols. (London: 1742)

Bourelly, Jules, *Cromwell et Mazarin; Deux Campagnes de Turenne en Flandre; la bataille des Dunes* (Paris: Perrin et cie, 1886)

Boyle, Roger, Lord Orrery, *Treatise of the Art of War* (1677)

British Library, Lansdowne MS

Firth, C. H. (ed.), *The Clarke papers. Selections from the papers of William Clarke, secretary to the Council of the Army, 1647-1649, and to General Monck and the commanders of the army in Scotland, 1651–1660* (London: Camden Society, 1891–1901)

Green, M. A. E. (ed.), *Calendar of State Papers, Domestic; Commonwealth Series, 1656–7* (London: 1883)

Green, M. A. E. (ed.), *Calendar of State Papers, Domestic Series, of the reign of Charles II. 1660-1661* (London: Longman et al., 1860)

Green, M. A. E. (ed.), *Calendar of State Papers, Domestic Series, of the reign of Charles II. 1661-1662* (London: Longman et al., 1861)

Heath, James, *A Chronicle of the Late Intestine War in the Three Kingdoms* (London: 1675)

Historical Manuscripts Commission, *The Manuscripts of the Marquis of Ormonde, preserved at the Castle, Kilkenny* (London: H. M. C., 1895)

Historical Manuscripts Commission, *The Manuscripts of J. Eliot Hodgkin, esq., F. S. A., of Richmond, Surrey* (London: for H. M. Stationery Office, 1897)

Macray, W. D. (ed.), *Calendar of the Clarendon State Papers preserved in the Bodleian Library*, vols. 3 and 4 (Oxford: Clarendon Press, 1872)

Macray, W. D. (ed.), Hyde, Edward, Earl of Clarendon, *The History of the Rebellion and Civil Wars in England begun in the year 1641* (Oxford, 1884)

Mercurius Politicus, London, 1657–8. Issues as footnoted.

Morgan, Sir Thomas, *The memoirs of Major-General Morgan. Containing a true and faithful relation of his progress in France and Flanders, with the six-thousand British forces, in the years 1657 and 1658* (Glasgow: R. Urie, 1752)

Sells, A. Lytton (ed.), *Memoirs of James II* (London: Chatto & Windus, 1962)

Tucker, Norman and Young, Peter (eds.), *The Civil War: Richard Atkyns and John Gwynne* (London: Longmans, 1967)

Wheatley, Henry B., *The Diary of Samuel Pepys*, 2 vols. (London: Random House, 1950)

Secondary Sources

von Arni, Eric Gruber, *Justice to the Maimed Soldier: nursing, medical care and welfare for sick and wounded soldiers and their families during the English Civil Wars and Interregnum, 1642–1660* (Aldershot: Ashgate, 2001)

Asquith, Stuart, and Warner, Chris, *New Model Army, 1645–1660* (London: Osprey, 1981)

Barratt, John, *Cromwell's Wars at Sea* (Barnsley: Pen & Sword Military, 2006)

Chartrand, René, *French Musketeer, 1622–1775* (Oxford: Osprey, 2015)

Firth, C. H., *The Last Years of the Protectorate, 1656–1658*, 2 vols. (London: Longmans, 1909)

BIBLIOGRAPHY

Firth, C. H. and Davies, Godfrey, *The Regimental History of Cromwell's Army*, Volume II (Oxford: Clarendon Press, 1940)

Gush, George, *Renaissance Armies, 1480–1650* (Cambridge: Patrick Stephens, 1982, 2nd ed.)

Hernández, Antonio José Rodríguez, *Breve historia de los Tercios de Flandes* (Madrid: Nowtilus, 2015)

Historical Manuscripts Commission, *Report on the manuscripts of F. W. Leyborne-Popham, Esq. of Littlecote, Co. Wilts* (London: H. M. C., 1902)

Jennings, Brendan, *Wild Geese in Spanish Flanders, 1588–1700* (Dublin: Stationery Office for the Irish Manuscripts Commission, 1964)

Longueville, Thomas, *Marshal Turenne* (London: Longman's Green, 1886)

López, Ignacio and Iván Notario, *The Spanish Tercios 1536–1704* (Oxford: Osprey, 2012)

The Oxford Dictionary of National Biography (Oxford: Oxford University Press, 2004)

Parker, Geoffrey, *The Army of Flanders and the Spanish Road, 1567–1659; the logistics of Spanish victory and defeat in the Low Countries' Wars* (Cambridge: Cambridge University Press, 1972)

Roberts, Keith, *Pike and Shot Tactics 1590–1660* (Oxford: Osprey, 2010)

Rodger, N. A. M., *The Command of the Ocean: A Naval History of Britain, 1649–1815* (London: Allen Lane, 2004)

Scott, Sir Sibald David, *The British Army, its Origin, Progress and Equipment* (London: Cassell, 1868)

Stanford, Iain. 'A study of Orders of Battle from the age of Louis XIV (1643-1715), No 1 – British Regiments at the Battle of the Dunes 4th/14th June 1658', *The Arquebusier*, volume 34, issue 3.

Woolrych, Austin, *Britain in Revolution* (Oxford: Oxford University Press, 2002)

Articles

Aylmer, G. E., 'Sir John Reynolds (1625–1657)', in *The Oxford Dictionary of National Biography* (Oxford: Oxford University Press, 2005)

Barratt, John, 'Adventures of Richard Grace', in *Military Illustrated*, 103, 2009

Firth, C. H., 'Royalist and Cromwellian Armies in Flanders' in *Transactions of the Royal Historical Society*, vol. 16 (London: Cambridge University Press for the Royal Historical Society, 1902)

Goulier, Pierre, 'Mercenaries Irelandais en Service de la France', in *Irish Sword*, 27, 1986–7

Morgan, Basil, 'Sir Thomas Morgan', in *The Oxford Dictionary of National Biography* (Oxford: Oxford University Press, 2004)

Venning, Timothy, 'Sir William Lockhart', in *The Oxford Dictionary of National Biography* (Oxford: Oxford University Press, 2004)

Index

Index of Places

Antwerp 25, 32
Ardres 41, 44-47, 49-50, 52
Arras 15, 23, 33
Artois 67-68

Beauvais 29, 118
Bergues 49, 50, 52, 68, 70, 104-105, 108
Boulogne 37-38, 48, 57, 59, 107
Bourbourg 52, 59-60, 67
Boutteville 76, 98
Bristol 23-24, 26, 29, 31-32, 35, 41, 64-65, 68, 80, 93, 98, 107, 118
Bruges 4, 20, 22, 25-26, 28, 30, 32, 103-104, 107
Brussels 31-32, 44, 65, 68-69, 71, 73, 75, 105

Cadiz 4, 8-10
Calais 12, 33, 37, 41-42, 48, 53, 59, 68, 72, 104, 112
Cambrai 47, 64, 68, 71
Catalonia 13, 26-27, 33

Deal 59, 117-118
Dixmude 65, 103-105
Dover 37-38, 57-58, 61
Dunkirk 4-5, 7-8, 10, 12-13, 16, 32-33, 47-50, 52-59, 62-66, 68, 70-73, 75, 77-78, 81-82, 101-104, 108-119

Flanders 4-5, 10, 12-18, 20-22, 24-26, 28, 31-34, 36, 40-42, 47-49, 57, 59, 61, 64, 67, 70, 80, 99, 103-104, 106, 108-109, 111-112, 114-117, 120
Fort Leon 71, 74, 101
Fort Royal 70-71, 78, 108
France 4-7, 12, 14-17, 19-21, 24, 26-29, 31, 33, 37-39, 41, 47-50, 60-62, 64, 69, 99, 102, 106-108, 112, 118, 120
Furnes 71, 73, 75-77, 80-82, 92, 97, 99, 103-104

Gloucester 18, 36
Gravelines 4, 42, 47-50, 52-53, 55, 63, 65-67, 72-73, 104-105, 108

Hesdin 67-68, 70

Ireland 17, 20, 23, 27, 35, 118
Italy 13-14, 21, 26, 33

Jamaica 8-9, 90

London 7, 9, 21-22, 32, 35-36, 49, 58-60, 102, 110-111, 115-116, 118, 120-121
Low Countries 12-13, 36, 121
Lys (River) 40, 42, 49, 70

Madrid 14, 121
Mardyke 4, 33, 47, 49-54, 56-57, 59-65, 67-68, 70-72, 78, 102, 108-109, 111, 116-118
Montmédy 40-42, 49

Netherlands 11-12, 14-15, 18-19, 23, 107
Nieuport 71-73, 75, 91, 100, 103-104, 108, 110

Ostend 4, 32, 65, 67-69, 101, 103-104, 111

Paris 15-16, 26, 33, 59, 62, 106, 111, 120
Plymouth 10, 117
Portugal 10, 13, 15, 33, 98
Pyrenees 4, 15, 33, 108

Santa Cruz 4, 10, 71

INDEX

Scotland 12, 18-19, 36, 120
Spain 3-10, 13-16, 18-21, 24, 27, 33, 45, 51, 67, 99, 102, 106-108, 112, 119
Spanish Flanders 20, 24, 33, 121
Spanish Netherlands 12, 14, 23, 107
St Ghislain 31-32, 35
St Omer 25, 42, 52, 68, 70, 102, 105, 107-108
St Quentin 40, 57
St Venant 4, 38, 40-42, 44-47, 49

West Indies 7, 9, 18

York 15, 21-22, 24-27, 29-32, 41-46, 50-57, 62, 64-65, 68, 70-71, 75-77, 79-80, 84, 86, 88, 90-93, 95, 97, 100, 103-105, 107, 116-118
Ypres 73, 75, 103, 105

Zudcote 75-76, 96

Index of People

Alsop, Colonel Roger 36, 84, 93, 109, 112-114, 119

Blake, General at Sea Robert 4, 8-10, 71

Caracena, Luis Francisco de Benavides Carrillo de Toledo, Marquis of 14-15, 23, 25-26, 29, 43-44, 46, 52, 54, 73, 75-77, 79, 88-89, 91, 96, 103-104, 107, 115
Castelnau, Marquis de 51, 70-71, 81, 84, 90-91
Charles I 19, 23
Charles II 4-6, 12-15, 18-20, 32, 34-35, 40, 47, 55-56, 62, 64-65, 67-68, 71, 80, 83, 93, 97, 99-100, 106, 108, 113-118, 120
Clarendon, Edward Hyde, Earl of 21-23, 25-29, 33-35, 55, 64-65, 107, 113, 120-121
Clarke, William 39-40, 47-48, 53, 55-57, 70, 73, 84-85, 90, 93, 97, 99, 104, 112, 120
Cochrane, Colonel Sir Bryce 36, 84, 104, 112
Condé, Prince de 13-17, 22, 33, 42, 44-46, 50, 68, 70, 75, 78, 80-81, 91-92, 97, 103-105
Cordpva, Don Antonio de 80, 98, 103
Cromwell, Henry 18, 35, 47, 62
Cromwell, Oliver, Lord Protector 4-11, 17-20, 22-24, 28, 33, 35-36, 47-49, 52, 59, 61-63, 66-67, 69, 73, 98, 102, 105, 107, 109-111, 113, 118, 120

d'Aumont, Marshal Antoine 62-63, 68-69
d'Hocquincourt, Charles de Moncy, Marquis 27, 68, 75, 77
d'Humières, Marquis 44, 51
de Condé, Prince Louis, Duc d'Enghien 13-15, 33, 42, 44, 45-46, 50-52, 54-55, 76-77, 80, 92, 95-96, 98
De Leyde, Marquis 70-71, 101-102

de Ligne, Claude Lamont, 3rd Prince 42-43, 52, 75, 91, 98, 103, 105
De Marsin, Monsieur 35, 51, 54
Digby, Lord George, Earl of Bristol 23-26, 28, 31, 35, 41, 64, 68, 80, 93, 98, 107, 118
Don Gaspar Boniface 80, 82, 85, 87-92, 96, 98
Don Juan (of Austria) 14, 25, 28-29, 35, 40, 42-46, 50, 52, 54-56, 64-65, 67, 73, 75-76, 78-80, 84, 88, 90, 96, 98-99, 103-105
Drummond, Colonel 90, 97, 99

Farrell, Colonel 31, 87, 98, 107, 116-118
Fenwick, Colonel George 85, 87-88, 90, 98, 102
Fleetwood, General John 6, 62

Gibbon, Colonel 61, 63, 67, 109
Godson, Vice Admiral William 53, 67, 72
Grace, Colonel Richard 23, 28-29, 31, 33-34, 80, 92, 96, 107, 116-118, 121
Gwynne, Lieutenant John 94, 100, 106, 114, 120

Harley, Colonel Sir Edward 114, 116, 118-119
Henry, Duke of Gloucester 24, 30-32, 41, 45-46, 54, 65, 70, 80, 89, 107-108, 116-118
Hughes, Lieutenant Colonel Richard 56, 70, 84-85, 88, 90, 93, 97, 104

James, Duke of York 15, 21-22, 24-27, 28-32, 35, 41-46, 50-57, 62, 64-65, 68, 70-71, 75-77, 79-81, 84, 86, 88, 90-93, 95-97, 100, 103-105, 107-108, 116-118, 120-1

Leyde, Marquis de 70-71, 101
Lillingston, Colonel Henry 90, 114
Lockhart, Sir William 18-19, 24-25, 39, 47-49,

125

57, 59-60, 62-64, 66-69, 71-73, 78, 82, 84-85, 87, 89, 91, 96-98, 101-102, 108-114, 118-119
Louis XIV 15, 33, 37, 40, 59, 70, 99, 102, 104

Marvell, Andrew 102-103
Mazarin, Cardinal 6-7, 16, 22-23, 26, 38-40, 47-49, 59-60, 63-64, 66-69, 72-73, 78, 92, 98, 102, 108-109, 111, 120
Middleton, Lieutenant-General 26, 31, 41, 93
Monck, General George 18, 36, 39, 47, 53, 93, 99, 112, 114, 120
Montagu, General at Sea Edward 9-10, 72
Montgomery, Monsieur de 19, 81, 92
Morgan, General Thomas 38, 41, 47, 63, 67, 82-86, 90, 104, 120
Muskerry, Colonel Lord 23, 31, 41

Newburgh, Lord 30-32, 41, 64, 80, 107, 116-118

Ormonde, Marquis of 21-23, 25, 30-34, 41, 55, 64, 120

Pepys, Samuel 113-114, 120

Peters, Hugh 36, 111, 113

Reynolds, General Sir John 17-19, 35-36, 38, 40-41, 47, 49, 57, 59, 61-63, 120-121
Richelieu, Cardinal Armand Jean du Plessis 15, 82, 101
Rutherford, Lord 115, 117-118

Schomberg, Compte de 73, 81, 90

Taaffe, Lieutenant Colonel Lord Theobald 26, 31, 35, 41, 64, 116, 118
Thurloe, Secretary John 9, 22-23, 30, 32, 54, 66, 120
Turenne, Marshal Henri de La Tour d'Auvergne 15-17, 21, 24, 33, 40-44, 46-47, 49, 50, 52, 55, 59, 60-61, 63, 69-74, 76-79, 81-85, 91-93, 96-101, 104-105, 107-109, 111

Venables, General Robert 8-9, 18

Walker, Sir Edward 28-29, 33
Wilmot, Lord 30, 32, 34, 41, 120

Index of Military Formations & Units

Anglo-French army 33, 81
Army of Flanders 4, 12-13, 17, 31, 34, 49, 80, 121

'Blue Regiment', Commonwealth 85-86

Commonwealth army 17, 35

Duke of Gloucester's Regiment 70, 107, 117
Duke of York's Regiment 30, 32, 70, 116-118

English Navy 6, 8, 66, 75

Foot Guards 92, 118
French army 15-16, 19, 33, 35, 40, 42, 44, 48-51, 57, 59, 64, 66, 78, 81, 91, 96, 99, 104
French Foot 63, 79, 99

Garde Française 59, 68-69, 72, 78, 81, 84, 91 102

Horse Guards 50, 76-77, 79-80, 117

Irish regiments 31-32, 70, 118

King's Regiment, The 15, 30-31, 71, 85, 88, 93-94, 98, 100, 107, 114-115, 117-118

Lillingston's Regiment, Colonel Henry 111-112, 119

Picardie regiment 16, 81, 91

'Redcoats' 5, 82, 96
Regiment of Guards 30, 64, 115
Regiments of Foot 15, 27, 30, 36, 47, 62, 71, 85, 93, 98, 100, 107, 109, 114, 117-118
Regiments of Horse 25, 27, 32, 92-93, 107, 109, 114, 119
Royalist Army 5, 12, 15, 20, 25, 29, 31, 47, 64, 106-108
Spanish Army 4, 13-15, 44, 49-51, 63-64, 80-81, 84, 88, 91

INDEX

Index of General & Miscellaneous Terms

Catalan Revolt 14, 33
Council of State, Commonwealth 6-7, 58, 113
Council of War, Spanish 14, 44-46, 75, 103

Dunes, Battle of the 4-5, 13-14, 57, 75, 83, 95, 102, 105, 107-108

English Civil Wars 12, 17-18, 26-27, 30, 35-36, 58, 120

Franco-Spanish War 4, 12, 16, 33, 108
French Civil Wars (the Fronde) 33

Irish Confederates 17, 20

Plate Fleet, Spanish 4, 9-10

Protectorate, The 5-7, 9, 17-18, 35, 120

Restoration of Charles II 4-5, 18, 36, 108, 113-114, 117, 119
Rocroi, Battle of 4, 12-13, 15, 17
Royalist uprising 18, 29
Royalists/Royalism 6, 13-15, 20-21, 26, 29-30, 33, 35, 57, 64, 68, 80, 83, 107-108, 113, 119

'Spanish Road' 12, 14, 17, 121

Tangiers 5, 95, 118-119
Thirty Years' War 12, 15-16, 36
Treaty of Bruges 4, 20
Treaty of the Pyrenees 4, 14, 108

'Western Design' 4, 7-9